A Journey into Wiccan Ethics

Alchemy of the Spirit: Discovering the Transformative Philosophy and Ethics of Wicca

Morgan Ravenwood

Table of Contents

INTRODUCTION

In the tapestry of human spirituality, a thread exists that weaves the ancient with the modern, the mystical with the practical, and the earthly with the divine. This thread is known as Wicca, a contemporary pagan, nature-based spiritual path that has captured the imagination and hearts of countless seekers worldwide. At its core, Wicca is not merely a set of rituals or beliefs; it is a profound philosophy and ethical framework that offers a unique perspective on life, nature, and the interconnectedness of all things.

"A Journey into Wiccan Ethics: Alchemy of the Spirit - Discovering the Transformative Philosophy and Ethics of Wicca" delves deep into the heart of Wicca, illuminating its origins, core beliefs, ethical principles, and practices that have enchanted and transformed the lives of its practitioners. This book serves as a comprehensive guide for both those new to Wicca and those seeking to deepen their understanding of this spiritual path.

Throughout these pages, we will explore the rich tapestry of Wiccan history, the intricate dance of its core beliefs, and the profound ethical code encapsulated in the Wiccan Rede. We will uncover the secrets of Wiccan rituals and practices, delving into the alchemical transformation of the self and our relationship with the natural world. Moreover, we will navigate Wicca's challenges and opportunities in today's diverse and interconnected world.

Join us on a journey of discovery where ancient wisdom meets modern sensibilities and where the alchemy of the spirit is the key to unlocking the transformative power of Wiccan philosophy and ethics. Whether you are a curious soul or a seasoned practitioner, this book invites you to explore the depths of Wicca's transformative magic and embrace the wisdom of its ethical foundations.

CHAPTER I

Origins and History of Wicca

The Roots of Wicca

Wicca, often described as a modern pagan, nature-based religion, is rooted in a complex tapestry of historical, cultural, and spiritual influences. To understand the origins of Wicca, one must embark on a journey that traverses centuries and continents, blending folklore, ancient practices, and the visionary insights of key individuals who shaped this contemporary spiritual path.

The roots of Wicca extend deep into the annals of human history. One of its foundational pillars is the reverence for nature and recognizing the divine in the natural world. This connection with nature has ancient origins, with echoes in prehistoric animistic beliefs, where every element of the natural world was imbued with spiritual significance. Wicca draws upon this ancestral veneration of nature, celebrating the cycles of the seasons, the phases of the moon, and the interconnectedness of all living beings.

Another significant influence on Wicca's roots is Western occultism, which saw a resurgence in the late 19th and early 20th centuries. Figures like Aleister Crowley and the Hermetic Order of the Golden Dawn played a pivotal role in shaping modern Wicca's magical and ritualistic aspects. Wiccan rituals, tools, and symbolism owe a debt to the Hermetic traditions, which sought to explore the hidden realms of spirituality and mysticism.

However, in the mid-20th century, Wicca emerged as a distinct and organized religious movement. Gerald Gardner, often called the "Father of Wicca," is a central figure in this development. In the 1950s, Gardner claimed to have been initiated into a surviving witchcraft tradition, which he later termed "Wica" or "Wicca." He codified its practices, incorporating elements of ceremonial magic, folklore, and his own insights into a cohesive system. Gardner's efforts resulted in the publication of books like "Witchcraft Today" and "The Meaning of Witchcraft," which introduced Wicca to a broader audience.

Doreen Valiente, often considered the "Mother of Wicca," collaborated with Gardner and significantly contributed to the Wiccan rituals and liturgy. Her poetic revisions and additions to the Book of Shadows, a sacred text in Wicca, added depth and beauty to the tradition. Valiente's work helped solidify Wicca's structure and ethics, emphasizing the Wiccan Rede: "An it harm none, do what thou wilt."

It is essential to recognize that while Gardner and Valiente played pivotal roles in formalizing Wicca as a religious tradition, they were not the sole architects. Wicca's development was, to some extent, a collective effort, with input from various individuals who shared an interest in reviving and modernizing witchcraft practices.

The roots of Wicca also extend into the realm of folklore and witch trials. The image of the witch, both feared and revered, has deep historical roots in Europe, particularly during the witch trials of the 16th and 17th centuries. While these trials were a dark period in history, they contributed to the mythology of the witch and, by extension, to modern witchcraft traditions, including Wicca. The witch's figure, as a practitioner of magic and a keeper of ancient wisdom, became a symbol of empowerment and resistance.

Moreover, the influence of indigenous and non-European spiritual traditions cannot be overlooked. Some elements of Wicca, such as the concept of the four elements, the use of herbs and crystals, and the practice of divination, bear similarities to indigenous beliefs and practices from various cultures worldwide. Wicca's syncretic nature allowed it to draw inspiration from diverse sources, creating a spiritual path that resonated with many seeking a deeper connection to the spiritual world.

In conclusion, the roots of Wicca are a complex blend of ancient nature reverence, Western occultism, visionary individuals like Gerald Gardner and Doreen Valiente, folklore and witch trials, and the global tapestry of spiritual traditions. Wicca's emergence as a modern pagan religion represents a revival and adaptation of ancient wisdom in the context of the 20th century. It is a testament to the enduring human quest for spiritual connection, empowerment, and a harmonious relationship with the natural world. Understanding these multifaceted roots enriches our appreciation of Wicca's unique place in the landscape of contemporary spirituality.

Influential Figures in Wicca's History

The history of Wicca, a modern pagan, nature-based religion, is replete with influential figures who have left an indelible mark on its development. Through their teachings, writings, and practices, these individuals have shaped Wicca into the diverse and vibrant spiritual path it is today. Exploring the lives and contributions of some of these influential figures provides valuable insights into the evolution of Wicca and its enduring appeal.

Gerald Gardner, often called the "Father of Wicca," occupies a central place in the annals of Wicca's history. Born in 1884 in England, Gardner claimed to have been initiated into a surviving witchcraft tradition in the New Forest region. In the 1950s, he introduced Wicca to a broader audience by publishing books like "Witchcraft

Today" and "The Meaning of Witchcraft." Gardner codified Wiccan rituals, introduced the "Book of Shadows" concept as a sacred text, and emphasized the importance of the Wiccan Rede: "An it harm none, do what thou wilt." His efforts played a pivotal role in shaping the modern practice of Wicca, and many Wiccan traditions trace their lineage back to Gardnerian Wicca.

Doreen Valiente, often regarded as the "Mother of Wicca," worked closely with Gerald Gardner and significantly contributed to developing Wiccan rituals and liturgy. Born in 1922 in England, Valiente's poetic revisions and additions to the Book of Shadows added depth and beauty to the tradition. Her influence can be seen in crafting Wiccan rituals, which she helped standardize and enrich. Valiente's commitment to preserving and evolving the craft's spiritual and ethical aspects ensured that Wicca remained a living and dynamic tradition.

Raymond Buckland, a prominent figure in the history of Wicca, played a crucial role in its spread to the United States. Born in England in 1934, Buckland was initiated into Gardnerian Wicca by Monique Wilson (Lady Olwen) and subsequently moved to the United States. He founded his own tradition, Seax-Wica, which adapted Wicca to American cultural and environmental contexts. Buckland's books, including "Witchcraft from the Inside" and "The Complete Book of Witchcraft," introduced Wicca to a broad American audience and inspired many to explore its practices.

Another influential figure in Wicca's history is Raymond's wife, Lady Rowan Buckland. She was instrumental in the development of Seax-Wica and played a significant role in the coven and community leadership. Her dedication to Wiccan education and the dissemination of Wiccan teachings helped foster the growth of Wicca in the United States.

Starhawk, whose birth name is Miriam Simos, has been a prominent voice in contemporary Wicca and neopaganism. Born in 1951 in the United States, she is a prolific author and activist known for her influential book "The Spiral Dance: A Rebirth of the Ancient Religion of the Great Goddess." Starhawk's writings emphasize the feminist and ecological aspects of Wicca, advocating for the empowerment of women and the importance of environmental stewardship within the tradition. Her work has contributed to the feminist spirituality movement and has inspired many to explore the spiritual dimensions of social and ecological activism.

Scott Cunningham, born in 1956 in the United States, was Wicca's well-known author and practitioner. His books, including "Wicca: A Guide for the Solitary Practitioner" and "Cunningham's Encyclopedia of Magical Herbs," made Wicca accessible to a broad audience. Cunningham's emphasis on self-initiation and solitary practice resonated with individuals seeking a more individualized and eclectic approach to Wicca. His work inspires solitary practitioners and those exploring a more personalized connection with Wiccan spirituality.

These influential figures, among many others, have played pivotal roles in developing and popularizing Wicca. Their dedication to preserving, evolving, and disseminating Wiccan teachings and practices has ensured that Wicca remains a thriving and diverse spiritual path. As Wicca continues to evolve and adapt in the modern world, these historical figures serve as beacons of inspiration for both newcomers and seasoned practitioners, emphasizing the enduring relevance and vitality of this unique pagan tradition.

Evolution of Wiccan Philosophy and Ethics

Wicca, a modern pagan, nature-based religion, is characterized not only by its rituals and practices but also by a distinctive philosophy and ethical framework. The evolution of Wiccan philosophy and ethics is a fascinating journey that reflects the interplay of historical, cultural, and spiritual influences. From its early roots to its contemporary manifestations, Wicca's ethical principles and philosophical underpinnings have undergone significant development.

At the heart of Wicca's philosophy is the veneration of nature and the belief in the interconnectedness of all living beings. This reverence for the natural world is deeply rooted in ancient animistic traditions, where every element of the environment, from trees to animals, was considered sacred and imbued with spiritual significance. Wicca's founders drew upon these ancient beliefs, integrating them into a modern spiritual framework. The Wheel of the Year, which celebrates the changing seasons and natural cycles, became a central element of Wiccan practice, emphasizing the profound connection between humanity and the natural world.

The early evolution of Wiccan philosophy was heavily influenced by Western occultism. Figures like Aleister Crowley and the Hermetic Order of the Golden Dawn played a significant role in shaping Wicca's magical and ritualistic aspects. Ceremonial magic, using tools, and casting circles were all integrated into Wiccan rituals. This blend of occultism and nature reverence gave birth to a unique fusion of spirituality that continues to define Wicca.

Gerald Gardner, often considered the founder of modern Wicca, played a pivotal role in codifying Wiccan philosophy and ethics. In the 1950s, Gardner introduced Wicca to a broader audience through his books, including "Witchcraft Today" and "The Meaning of Witchcraft." He emphasized the importance of personal responsibility and the ethical principle encapsulated in the Wiccan Rede: "An it harm none, do what thou wilt." This maxim, often interpreted as advocating for actions that do not cause harm, became a cornerstone of Wiccan ethics. Gardner's efforts solidified Wicca's moral compass, providing a clear ethical framework for its practitioners.

Doreen Valiente, a close collaborator of Gerald Gardner and a prominent figure in Wiccan history, contributed significantly to the evolution of Wiccan philosophy and ethics. Her poetic revisions and additions to the Book of Shadows, a sacred text in Wicca, infused the tradition with depth and beauty. Valiente's contributions enriched Wicca's spiritual and ethical aspects, ensuring that its philosophy resonated on both intellectual and emotional levels.

As Wicca continued to evolve, it absorbed influences from other spiritual traditions and philosophies. The feminist movement of the 1960s and 1970s, in particular, profoundly impacted Wicca's ethical framework. Wicca, emphasizing the divine feminine and gender equality, aligned closely with feminist values. Many women found empowerment and a sense of agency in Wicca, and the tradition became a platform for exploring gender roles, sexuality, and the reclamation of female spiritual authority.

The 1980s and 1990s witnessed a surge of interest in environmentalism and ecological ethics, which found a natural home within Wicca. The belief in the sacredness of nature and the need for its preservation resonated strongly with the growing environmental consciousness of the era. Wiccan ethics, emphasizing harmlessness and responsible stewardship of the Earth, aligned perfectly with the emerging environmental movement. Many Wiccans actively integrated environmental concerns into their spiritual practices, further expanding the ethical dimensions of the tradition.

The 21st century has brought further evolution to Wiccan philosophy and ethics. With the advent of the internet and the global exchange of ideas, Wicca has become increasingly diverse and eclectic. Modern practitioners can draw inspiration from various sources, adapting and personalizing their ethical and philosophical perspectives. This diversity has given rise to various branches and traditions within Wicca, each with its unique interpretation of Wiccan philosophy and ethics.

In recent years, there has also been a growing emphasis on inclusivity and social justice within some Wiccan circles. This evolution reflects a broader societal awareness of diversity, equality, and human rights issues. Some Wiccans have expanded their ethical concerns to include social justice activism, aligning their spiritual beliefs with a commitment to addressing systemic inequalities and fostering greater inclusivity within the tradition.

In conclusion, the evolution of Wiccan philosophy and ethics is a testament to the adaptability and resilience of this modern pagan tradition. From its ancient animistic roots to its fusion with Western occultism, from the codification of ethical principles by Gerald Gardner to the feminist and environmental movements of the 20th century, Wicca has continually evolved to reflect the changing spiritual and ethical landscape. As it continues to evolve in the 21st century, Wicca remains a dynamic and relevant spiritual path, offering a unique philosophical and ethical perspective that resonates with individuals seeking a deeper connection with nature, themselves, and the divine.

The Wiccan Rede

The Wiccan Rede is one of the central ethical principles in Wicca, a modern pagan, nature-based religion. Often encapsulated in the phrase, "An it harm none, do what thou wilt," the Rede is a foundational guideline for Wiccan practitioners in their moral and ethical decision-making.

The origins and interpretation of the Wiccan Rede are complex, reflecting the rich tapestry of Wicca's history and philosophy. This essay explores the history, significance, and diverse interpretations of the Wiccan Rede within contemporary Wiccan practice.

The Wiccan Rede, despite its concise formulation, carries profound ethical implications. At its core, it advocates for actions that do not cause harm to others or oneself. This principle aligns with the broader Wiccan belief in the interconnectedness of all living beings and the sacredness of nature. By adhering to the Rede, Wiccans aim to live in harmony with their surroundings and foster a sense of responsibility toward their magical and mundane actions. The origins of the Wiccan Rede are somewhat elusive, and its precise lineage is challenging to trace. Some claim that it can be found in earlier forms within Western esoteric traditions, such as the writings of Aleister Crowley, where the phrase "Do what thou wilt shall be the whole of the Law" appears. However, as it is known today, the specific formulation of the Wiccan Rede can be attributed to the mid-20th century and the influence of Gerald Gardner, considered the father of modern Wicca. Gardner introduced the Rede in his books, "Witchcraft Today" and "The Meaning of Witchcraft," in the 1950s.

One interpretation of the Wiccan Rede is that it grants practitioners a degree of personal freedom and autonomy while emphasizing ethical responsibility. The phrase "do what thou wilt" is often understood not as a license for reckless or harmful behavior but as an invitation to self-discovery and authentic living. In this view, the Rede encourages individuals to explore their true selves, pursue their passions, and embrace their unique paths, provided that these actions do not cause harm to others. It advocates for a balance between personal liberty and ethical consideration.

However, the simplicity of the Wiccan Rede has also led to diverse interpretations and debates within the Wiccan community. Some argue that the Rede is overly simplistic and does not provide clear guidance in complex moral situations. They point out that determining what constitutes harm can be subjective and context-dependent. For example, is it harmful to perform a spell that influences another person's free will, even if the intention is benevolent? Such questions have sparked discussions among Wiccans about the practical application and boundaries of the Rede.

Variations of the Wiccan Rede have emerged to address some of these complexities. One such variation is the "Threefold Law," which suggests that the energy or intention one puts into the world, whether positive or negative, will return to them threefold. This concept adds a layer of karmic consequences to one's actions and encourages practitioners to consider the potential repercussions of their deeds more carefully. While the Threefold Law is not universally accepted among all Wiccans, it offers a more nuanced perspective on the ethical implications of magical and mundane actions.

Another aspect of the Wiccan Rede that has generated discussion is the word "none." Critics argue that it is nearly impossible to live a life without causing any harm whatsoever, as harm can be unintentional or unavoidable in some cases. This raises questions about the practicality of the Rede and how rigorously it should be followed. Some Wiccans interpret the Rede in a way that acknowledges the inherent challenges of avoiding all harm, emphasizing the intention to minimize harm and make amends when necessary.

In recent years, there has been a growing emphasis within some Wiccan circles on social justice and activism as an extension of the ethical principles embodied in the Rede. Some practitioners argue that addressing systemic inequalities, advocating for environmental sustainability, and working for social justice align with the spirit of "harm none." This perspective broadens the Rede's application to encompass personal conduct and collective responsibility for creating a more just and harmonious world.

In conclusion, the Wiccan Rede is a foundational ethical principle in Wicca, offering guidance to practitioners in their moral and magical endeavors. Its origins in the mid-20th century and its concise formulation have led to diverse interpretations and debates within the Wiccan community. While some view it as a simple yet profound guideline for ethical living, others grapple with its practical application and boundaries in complex situations. Despite these challenges, the Wiccan Rede remains a central tenet of Wiccan spirituality, inspiring practitioners to navigate the intricate balance between personal freedom and ethical responsibility in their spiritual journeys.

CHAPTER II

Core Beliefs in Wicca

The Divine and the Goddess

Wicca, a modern pagan, nature-based religion, holds a unique and profound perspective on the divine, embracing the sacred feminine in its understanding of the divine and the concept of the Goddess. In contrast to many monotheistic religions, Wicca celebrates a dualistic view of deity, incorporating both the God and the Goddess into its core beliefs and practices. This section explores the significance of the divine and the Goddess in Wiccan spirituality, shedding light on the rich tapestry of symbolism, mythology, and reverence surrounding the feminine aspect of the divine.

Central to Wiccan theology is the belief in a dual deity, consisting of the God and the Goddess. These two aspects are often seen as complementary and interdependent, representing the universe's balance of masculine and feminine energies. As a representation of the sacred feminine, the Goddess embodies a multiplicity of roles, archetypes, and qualities. She is the Great Mother, the Earth Mother, the Creatrix, the Warrior, the Lover, and the Crone, among others. This multifaceted portrayal of the Goddess reflects the diversity of human experience and the cyclical nature of life, death, and rebirth.

One of the most iconic symbols associated with the Goddess in Wicca is the Triple Goddess, representing the three phases of a woman's life and the lunar cycle: the Maiden, the Mother, and the Crone. The Maiden embodies youth, innocence, and the waxing moon; the Mother symbolizes fertility, nurturing, and the full moon; and the Crone represents wisdom, transformation, and the waning moon. The Triple Goddess is a potent symbol of the cyclical nature of existence, the seasons, and the ebb and flow of life's energies.

The veneration of the Goddess is not confined to mythology and symbolism; it permeates Wiccan rituals and practices. Many Wiccan rituals are dedicated to the Goddess, and her presence is invoked to bless and empower magical workings. The moon's cycles, so central to Wiccan observances, are often linked to the phases of the Goddess, and rituals are timed to align with these lunar rhythms. For example, the full moon is a time of celebrating the Mother aspect of the Goddess, while the new moon is associated with the Maiden.

The Goddess's connection to nature is another crucial aspect of her significance in Wicca. She is often seen as the embodiment of the Earth, and her cycles parallel the seasons. As the Earth changes and transforms throughout the year, so does the Goddess in her various forms. This deep connection to nature inspires Wiccans to honor and protect the environment, viewing it as an extension of the divine presence of the Goddess.

The Goddess's role as the Great Mother extends to her nurturing and protective qualities. Wiccans often turn to her for comfort, guidance, and healing. In times of distress or personal challenges, they seek solace in her loving and compassionate embrace. This maternal aspect of the Goddess provides a source of strength and resilience to Wiccans, reminding them of their connection to the divine and its support.

The concept of the Goddess in Wicca also challenges and redefines traditional gender roles and power structures. In a world where patriarchal systems have often dominated religious and societal institutions, the Goddess serves as a powerful symbol of female empowerment and spirituality. She stands as a reminder of the intrinsic value and sacredness of the feminine, encouraging gender equality and honoring women's roles and experiences.

The veneration of the Goddess in Wicca has also contributed to the resurgence of interest in goddess spirituality and feminist spirituality movements. Many women and some men find in the Goddess a source of inspiration, empowerment, and a reconnection with their own inner strength and wisdom. Goddess-centered spirituality has become a platform for exploring issues related to gender, identity, and spirituality, fostering a sense of community and shared values among its practitioners.

In conclusion, the concept of the divine and the Goddess in Wicca offers a unique and profound perspective on spirituality. Through symbolism, mythology, and ritual practice, the Goddess embodies the sacred feminine, celebrating diversity, the cycles of life, and the interconnectedness of all things. Her presence in Wiccan spirituality challenges traditional gender norms and inspires a sense of empowerment, reverence for nature, and a deep connection to the divine. As Wicca continues to evolve and adapt in the modern world, the Goddess remains a central and enduring symbol of the sacred feminine within the tapestry of this vibrant and dynamic spiritual tradition.

The Wheel of the Year

Central to the practice of Wicca, a modern pagan, nature-based religion, is the Wheel of the Year. This sacred calendar, consisting of eight festivals spaced throughout the year, marks the changing seasons and celebrates the natural cycles of life, death, and rebirth. The Wheel of the Year is a cornerstone of Wiccan spirituality, connecting practitioners to the rhythms of the Earth and the ever-turning wheel of existence. This section explores the significance of the Wheel of the Year in Wicca, delving into the meaning and rituals associated with each of its eight festivals.

The Wheel of the Year begins with the festival of Samhain, which is celebrated on October 31st or November 1st in the Northern Hemisphere. Samhain marks the end of the agricultural year and the beginning of the darker half of the year. It is a time when the veil between the physical and spiritual worlds is believed to be thin, making it an ideal moment for divination, ancestor veneration, and reflection on mortality. Samhain also serves as a time to bid farewell to the old and welcome the new, as the year transitions into the wintery months.

Yule, typically celebrated around December 21st in the Northern Hemisphere, is the winter solstice festival. It marks the longest night and the return of the sun's light, symbolizing the hope and promise of rebirth. Yule traditions often include lighting a Yule log, decorating evergreen trees, and exchanging gifts. It is a time of joy, community, and celebrating the triumph of light over darkness.

Imbolc, held around February 1st or 2nd, heralds the first signs of spring. This festival honors the Celtic goddess Brigid and celebrates the awakening of the Earth from its winter slumber. Imbolc is a time of purification and preparation, symbolized by lighting candles and crafting Brigid's crosses. It signifies the gradual return of life and fertility to the land.

Ostara, usually observed on March 20th or 21st, coincides with the vernal equinox, when day and night are of equal length. It celebrates balance and renewal, as nature awakens from its winter dormancy. Ostara customs include the coloring of eggs and the planting of seeds, symbolizing new beginnings and the fertility of the Earth. The goddess Eostre, from whom the festival derives its name, represents the dawn and the burgeoning light of spring.

Beltane, occurring on April 30th or May 1st, is a joyful and exuberant festival that marks the arrival of summer. It celebrates fertility, love, and the union of the God and the Goddess. Maypole dancing, bonfires, and the weaving of flower crowns are common Beltane customs. It is a time when the Earth is bursting with life, and the energies of creation are at their peak.

Litha, or the summer solstice, occurs around June 20th or 21st. It is the longest day of the year and a celebration of the sun's zenith. Litha honors the fullness of life and the abundance of the Earth. Bonfires, outdoor rituals, and the gathering of medicinal herbs are customary activities. Litha reminds Wiccans of the importance of balance as the sun's power begins to wane and the days gradually grow shorter.

Lammas, celebrated on August 1st or 2nd, marks the year's first harvest. It is a time to give thanks for the abundance of the Earth and to recognize the sacrifice of the God, who begins to weaken as the harvest is gathered. Baking bread, making corn dollies, and sharing communal feasts are typical Lammas customs. The festival underscores the interconnectedness of life and death, growth and decline.

Mabon, the autumnal equinox, occurs around September 21st or 22nd. It is a time of balance when day and night are once again of equal length. Mabon celebrates the second harvest and the preparation for the coming winter months. Activities include making cider, offering thanks, and honoring the God and Goddess as they prepare for their journey into the underworld.

With its eight festivals, the Wheel of the Year weaves a tapestry of spiritual significance and reverence for the natural world in Wicca. It provides a framework for

Wiccans to connect with the Earth's cycles, mark life's milestones, and deepen their relationship with the divine. Each festival offers unique opportunities for reflection, ritual, and celebration, reinforcing the central belief in the interconnectedness of all things and the sacredness of nature. Through the Wheel of the Year, Wiccans find a spiritual path that harmonizes with the rhythms of the Earth and allows them to embrace the ever-turning wheel of existence with gratitude, reverence, and a deep sense of connection to the natural world.

The Elements and Their Significance

Wicca, a modern pagan, nature-based religion, greatly emphasizes the natural world and the interconnectedness of all living beings. Central to Wiccan spirituality are the five elements: Earth, Air, Fire, Water, and Spirit. These elements serve as fundamental building blocks of the physical and spiritual realms, representing aspects of nature and human experience and consciousness. In this section, we will explore the significance of the elements in Wicca, their symbolism, and their role in rituals and magical practices.

Earth, the first of the five elements, symbolizes stability, fertility, and the physical realm. It is associated with the North and the material aspects of life. Earth represents the tangible, the practical, and the grounding force that connects us to the physical world. In Wiccan rituals, practitioners may call upon the element of Earth to provide stability, strength, and abundance. Salt, stones, and soil are often used to represent Earth on the Wiccan altar, serving as a focal point for grounding and centering.

Air, the element of intellect and communication, represents the East. It symbolizes clarity, thought, and the power of the mind. Air is associated with inspiration, knowledge, and the realm of ideas. In Wiccan rituals, it is invoked to aid in mental clarity, communication, and the flow of ideas. Feathers, incense smoke, or a wand may be used to represent Air on the altar, serving as a conduit for mental and spiritual energy.

Fire, residing in the South, embodies transformation, passion, and the force of will. It represents the spark of creativity, desire, and the energy needed for change. Fire is often invoked for courage, motivation, and manifesting one's intentions. In rituals, candles, a cauldron with a controlled flame, or a symbolic athame (ritual knife) may be used to symbolize Fire, allowing practitioners to tap into its transformative energy.

Water, associated with the West, represents emotions, intuition, and the subconscious realm. It symbolizes the ebb and flow of emotions, the depths of the psyche, and the cleansing power of emotions and intuition. Water is invoked for healing, purification, and psychic insight. In Wiccan rituals, a chalice filled with water, a consecrated bowl, or a seashell may be used to represent Water, serving as a conduit for emotional and intuitive energy.

The fifth element, Spirit, is often regarded as the divine source that binds all the other elements together. It represents the connection between the physical and spiritual realms and the divine spark within all living beings. Spirit transcends the limitations of space and time and is invoked to provide balance, harmony, and a sense of unity in rituals. While Spirit itself may not be symbolized on the Wiccan altar, it infuses all elements and aspects of the tradition, serving as a reminder of the interconnectedness of all things.

The elements play a significant role in Wiccan rituals and magical practices. Many Wiccan rituals begin by invoking the elemental quarters, calling upon the powers and qualities associated with each element to create a sacred and protected space. This practice, often known as "casting a circle," reinforces the idea of drawing upon the elemental forces for guidance, protection, and support during ritual work.

In spellcraft and magic, the elements are harnessed to enhance the effectiveness of spells and rituals. For example, if one were performing a ritual for prosperity, they might incorporate Earth elements, such as burying a crystal or herb in the ground, to symbolize growth and abundance. Similarly, if seeking inspiration or clarity, Air elements like incense may be used to promote clear thinking and communication.

The significance of the elements in Wicca extends beyond the rituals and magical workings. They serve as a spiritual framework that encourages practitioners to recognize and honor the interconnectedness of all living beings and the natural world. This recognition aligns with the core Wiccan belief in the sacredness of nature and the importance of living in harmony with the Earth.

Furthermore, the elements are often associated with specific qualities and attributes that mirror human experiences and emotions. Wiccans aim to gain a deeper understanding of themselves and their connection to the world around them by working with the elements. For example, Earth may be invoked to provide stability during times of uncertainty, while Fire may be called upon to fuel one's passions and motivation.

In conclusion, the elements hold profound significance in Wicca, foundational to its spirituality, rituals, and magical practices. They symbolize the natural world and the rich tapestry of human experience and consciousness. Wiccans seek to connect with the energies and qualities they represent by working with the elements, fostering a deeper connection to the Earth, the self, and the divine. The elements remind Wiccans of their place within the interconnected web of existence, reinforcing the central belief that all life is sacred and deserving of reverence.

The Concept of Magic in Wicca

Magic is a central and defining element of Wicca, a modern pagan, nature-based religion that celebrates the interconnectedness of all living beings and the sacredness of nature. In Wicca, magic is seen as a transformation, empowerment, and spiritual growth tool. This section explores the concept of magic in Wicca, its significance, and how it is practiced within the tradition.

At its core, magic in Wicca is the art of consciously and intentionally working with natural and spiritual energies to create change in accordance with one's will. Wiccans believe that everything in the universe is connected by a web of energy, and through rituals, spells, and other magical practices, they seek to tap into and manipulate these energies to achieve specific goals. Magic in Wicca is not viewed as supernatural or outside the realm of the natural world but as a natural and inherent part of human experience.

One of the fundamental principles of magic in Wicca is the belief that like attracts like, often summarized in the phrase "As above, so below; as below, so above." This principle, known as the Law of Correspondence, suggests that the individual's microcosm mirrors the universe's macrocosm, and changes made within the individual can influence the external world. Therefore, magic in Wicca often involves aligning one's thoughts, emotions, and intentions with their desired outcomes.

Magic is practiced in various forms within Wicca, and its methods can vary among individual practitioners and traditions. Some standard magical practices in Wicca include spellwork, divination, meditation, and the use of magical tools such as wands, athames (ritual knives), candles, herbs, crystals, and tarot cards. Each of these practices serves a specific purpose within Wiccan magic, whether for healing, protection, manifestation, or spiritual insight.

Spells, in particular, are a well-known aspect of Wiccan magic. A spell is a ritual that employs specific words, actions, and correspondences to focus and direct magical energy toward a particular goal. Spells can range from simple and everyday actions to elaborate and ceremonial rituals. Intent, visualization, and the manipulation of energy play crucial roles in the effectiveness of spells. Wiccans often emphasize the ethical use of magic, adhering to the ethical principle encapsulated in the Wiccan Rede: "An it harm none, do what thou wilt."
The timing of magical work is also significant in Wicca.

Many Wiccans consider the phases of the moon, the day of the week, and the seasons to be influential factors in determining when to perform certain spells or rituals. For example, spells for manifestation or growth might be conducted during the waxing moon, while banishing or releasing spells could be performed during the waning moon.
The concept of the sacred circle is fundamental to Wiccan magical practice. Before performing magic or rituals, Wiccans often cast a circle before performing magic or rituals, a symbolic and energetic boundary separating the sacred space from the mundane world. This circle serves multiple purposes: it provides protection, enhances the focus of energy, and creates a container for magical work. Within the circle, practitioners are in closer connection with the divine, the elements, and their own inner power.

The concept of magic in Wicca extends beyond the realm of spellwork and rituals. Wiccans view magic as an integral part of daily life, encompassing everyday acts of mindfulness, intention, and connection with the natural world. Whether it's blessing a meal, grounding and centering before a stressful day, or offering gratitude to nature, Wiccans seek to infuse their lives with a sense of magic and spiritual awareness.

The significance of magic in Wicca goes beyond its practical applications. It serves as a means of personal and spiritual growth, fostering a deeper connection to the self, the divine, and the interconnected web of existence. Through magical practices, Wiccans explore their own inner potential, confront and transform personal challenges, and cultivate a sense of empowerment and self-mastery.

Additionally, magic in Wicca reinforces the reverence for nature and the belief in the sacredness of the Earth. By working with the elements, seasons, and natural correspondences, Wiccans deepen their connection to the natural world and recognize their role as stewards of the Earth. This ecological consciousness is a central aspect of Wiccan spirituality and aligns with the tradition's commitment to living harmoniously with the environment.

In conclusion, the concept of magic in Wicca is a multifaceted and integral aspect of the tradition. It encompasses a range of practices and techniques that allow practitioners to work with natural and spiritual energies to create positive change and spiritual growth. Magic in Wicca is deeply rooted in the interconnectedness of all things and reflects the belief that the individual has the power to shape their reality and destiny. It serves as a means of self-discovery, empowerment, and communion with the divine while reinforcing the importance of ethical and ecological awareness within the tradition.

CHAPTER III

Ethics in Wicca

The Threefold Law

The Threefold Law is a foundational concept in Wicca, a modern pagan, nature-based religion that emphasizes the interconnectedness of all living beings and the importance of ethical conduct. Also known as the Law of Three or the Rule of Three, this principle posits that whatever energy or intention a person puts out into the world—whether through thoughts, words, or actions—will return to them threefold. In other words, the consequences of one's actions, be they positive or negative, will be magnified and reflected back upon the individual. This section explores the significance of the Threefold Law in Wicca, its ethical implications, and its role in shaping the behavior and worldview of Wiccans.

Central to the Threefold Law is the idea of cause and effect, which lies at the heart of many spiritual and philosophical traditions. Wiccans believe every action has a reaction and that the energy one sends into the universe eventually returns to influence their life. This concept echoes the law of karma in Eastern spiritual traditions, which suggests that one's actions have consequences that manifest in this life or in future incarnations. In Wicca, the Threefold Law serves as a reminder that individuals are responsible for their choices and their impact on others and the world around them.

The Threefold Law is often summarized in the phrase "Whatever you send out, returns to thee times three." This means that if a person engages in positive and benevolent actions, such as acts of kindness, love, or healing, the positive energy they generate will return to them in greater abundance. Conversely, if one engages in harmful or negative actions, such as deceit, harm, or ill will, the negative energy they send out will return with three times the force. This principle encourages Wiccans to be mindful of their actions and intentions, as they directly influence the quality of their lives.

Ethical considerations are paramount in Wicca, and the Threefold Law is crucial in shaping Wiccan ethics. Wiccans adhere to the ethical principle encapsulated in the Wiccan Rede: "An it harm none, do what thou wilt." This maxim emphasizes the importance of personal responsibility and the avoidance of harm to oneself and others. The Threefold Law complements the Wiccan Rede by highlighting the karmic consequences of one's actions. It encourages practitioners to consider their choices' potential effects and strive for ethical behavior.

The Threefold Law also underscores the importance of intention in magical and spiritual practices. Wiccans believe that intention is a powerful force that shapes the outcome of magical workings and rituals. Therefore, when performing spells or rituals, one must ensure that one's intentions are clear, positive, and aligned with the principles of harmlessness and ethical responsibility. This emphasis on intention cultivates mindfulness and personal growth, as practitioners learn to align their will with their ethical values.

Critics of the Threefold Law argue that it oversimplifies the complex nature of cause and effect, attributing all outcomes to a simple threefold return. They contend that the world does not always operate in such a straightforward manner and that the law can lead to a deterministic view of karma. Some argue that life's circumstances and consequences are influenced by numerous individual and collective factors, making it challenging to predict how energy will return.

Despite these criticisms, the Threefold Law remains a central and influential concept in Wicca. It serves as a moral compass, guiding Wiccans' choices and behaviors. Moreover, it fosters a sense of personal accountability, reminding practitioners that their actions have repercussions for themselves and the world around them. The Threefold Law reinforces the interconnectedness of all living beings and underscores the importance of living in harmony with nature and with one's fellow beings.

The Threefold Law also extends beyond personal ethics and into the realm of social responsibility. Some Wiccans interpret the law to mean that their actions can have a ripple effect in the broader world, influencing societal and environmental outcomes. This perspective encourages Wiccans to engage in acts of kindness, charity, and environmental stewardship, believing that the positive energy generated through such actions can contribute to a more harmonious and balanced world.

In conclusion, the Threefold Law is a fundamental and enduring concept in Wicca, shaping the tradition's ethical framework and influencing its practitioners' behavior and mindset. It underscores the importance of cause and effect, emphasizing the karmic consequences of one's actions and intentions. While some may view the law as overly simplistic or deterministic, it remains a powerful and meaningful principle in Wiccan spirituality, encouraging personal responsibility, ethical conduct, and a deeper understanding of the interconnectedness of all life. Ultimately, the Threefold Law is a guiding principle that empowers Wiccans to live in harmony with themselves, the natural world, and the greater cosmic order.

Harm None: The Ethical Foundation

Wicca, a modern pagan, nature-based religion, is guided by a foundational ethical principle encapsulated in the phrase "An it harm none, do what thou wilt." This maxim, known as the Wiccan Rede, serves as the ethical compass for Wiccans, shaping their beliefs, behaviors, and interactions with the world around them. In this section, we will explore the significance of the Wiccan Rede, its ethical implications, and how it influences the moral framework of Wicca.

The Wiccan Rede is a concise yet profound statement that encapsulates the essence of Wiccan ethics. It can be interpreted as an invitation to live authentically, embracing one's true self and desires, provided that these actions do not cause harm to oneself or others. At its core, the Rede emphasizes personal freedom and autonomy while simultaneously advocating for ethical responsibility. It encourages individuals to align their will with their ethical values and to consider the consequences of their actions on the well-being of all living beings.
The concept of "harm none" is central to the Wiccan Rede. It reflects the belief in all life's interconnectedness and nature's sacredness. Wiccans view every living being, whether human, animal, plant, or the Earth itself, as deserving of respect and protection from harm. This reverence for life extends to the understanding that harm can take various forms, including physical, emotional, or spiritual, and that all forms of harm should be avoided whenever possible.

With its emphasis on harmlessness, the Wiccan Rede aligns with the broader Wiccan belief in living in harmony with nature. Wicca celebrates the cycles of the seasons, the phases of the moon, and the rhythms of the Earth, acknowledging the inherent wisdom and sacredness of the natural world. By adhering to the Rede, Wiccans strive to ensure that their actions respect and protect the environment, acknowledging their role as stewards of the Earth.

While the Wiccan Rede provides a clear ethical guideline, its application can be complex and nuanced. Wiccans recognize that life often presents situations with competing interests and potential for harm. Therefore, practitioners engage in ongoing ethical reflection and strive to make choices that minimize harm and align with their values. This process involves considering the potential consequences of one's actions, evaluating intentions, and seeking to find solutions that prioritize harm reduction.

The Wiccan Rede is not a rigid moral code but a principle that encourages thoughtful and responsible decision-making. It acknowledges that ethical choices are not always black and white, and that individuals may find themselves facing dilemmas that require careful consideration. This flexibility allows Wiccans to navigate complex moral situations and make choices that reflect their commitment to harmlessness and personal responsibility.

Critics of the Wiccan Rede argue that it can be overly simplistic and idealistic, suggesting that it is nearly impossible to live a life without causing any harm whatsoever. They contend that intentional or unintentional harm is inherent in human existence and that striving for complete harmlessness is an unattainable goal. In response, some Wiccans interpret the Rede in a way that acknowledges the inherent challenges of avoiding all harm, emphasizing the intention to minimize harm and make amends when necessary.

The ethical foundation of the Wiccan Rede extends beyond individual conduct to include broader social and environmental concerns. Some Wiccans interpret the Rede as a call to engage in social justice and activism, viewing it as a way to address systemic inequalities, advocate for environmental sustainability, and promote ethical living on a collective level. This perspective expands the Rede's application to encompass personal conduct and collective responsibility for creating a more just and harmonious world.

In conclusion, the Wiccan Rede serves as the ethical cornerstone of Wicca, guiding practitioners in their moral and ethical decision-making. It embodies the belief in the interconnectedness of all life and the sacredness of nature, encouraging individuals to live in harmony with themselves, the natural world, and the greater cosmic order. While the Rede's emphasis on harmlessness is not without its complexities and challenges, it remains a central and enduring principle in Wiccan spirituality. Through the Wiccan Rede, practitioners find a moral framework that empowers them to navigate the intricate balance between personal freedom and ethical responsibility, fostering a deep sense of connection to the natural world and a commitment to a life lived with reverence and respect for all living beings.

Balancing Personal Freedom with Responsibility

Wicca, a modern pagan, nature-based religion, is renowned for its commitment to personal freedom and autonomy, encapsulated in the ethical principle "An it harm none, do what thou wilt." This principle, known as the Wiccan Rede, encourages individuals to live authentic lives, pursue their desires, and make choices that align with their true selves. However, this quest for personal freedom is tempered by the ethical responsibility of avoiding harm to oneself and others. Balancing personal freedom with responsibility is a central ethical dilemma in Wicca, which challenges practitioners to navigate the complexities of life's moral choices and the impact of their actions on the world around them.

Wicca's emphasis on personal freedom stems from its belief in individual empowerment and self-discovery. Wiccans celebrate the individual's autonomy and the recognition that each person's path is unique. They reject rigid dogma and religious authority, encouraging practitioners to explore their spirituality in ways that resonate with their inner selves. This emphasis on personal freedom fosters a sense of self-empowerment and self-realization, allowing individuals to embrace their true identities and desires.

At the heart of this freedom lies the principle "do what thou wilt," which encourages individuals to follow their will and passions. This concept does not promote reckless or impulsive behavior but instead advocates for the pursuit of one's true purpose and desires responsibly and ethically. It implies that individuals can make choices that align with their higher selves, provided those choices do not cause harm to others or oneself.

However, this pursuit of personal freedom in Wicca is not without its challenges. The ethical responsibility articulated in the Wiccan Rede tempers personal freedom with a commitment to harmlessness. This principle highlights the interconnectedness of all life and the importance of avoiding actions that may cause physical, emotional, or spiritual harm. The balance between personal freedom and responsibility requires practitioners to consider the consequences of their actions on the well-being of all living beings.

One of the ethical challenges within Wicca lies in determining what constitutes harm and how to minimize it. The concept of harm is subjective and can vary from person to person. Some actions that may seem harmless to one individual may be perceived as harmful by another. Therefore, Wiccans engage in ongoing ethical reflection, striving to make choices that minimize harm and align with their values. This process involves evaluating intentions, considering potential consequences, and seeking to find solutions that prioritize harm reduction.

Critics of the Wiccan Rede argue that it can be overly idealistic and simplistic, suggesting that it is nearly impossible to live without causing harm. They contend that intentional or unintentional harm is inherent in human existence and that striving for complete harmlessness is an unattainable goal. In response, some Wiccans interpret the Rede in a way that acknowledges the inherent challenges of avoiding all harm, emphasizing the intention to minimize harm and make amends when necessary.

Balancing personal freedom with responsibility also extends to the broader world and environmental concerns. Wiccans who embrace an ecological perspective view their commitment to harmlessness as an imperative for environmental stewardship. They recognize that human actions can cause harm to the Earth and its ecosystems, and they strive to live in harmony with nature. This perspective expands the ethical dilemma to include collective responsibility for addressing environmental challenges and advocating for sustainability.

In conclusion, the ethical dilemma of balancing personal freedom with responsibility lies at the heart of Wicca's moral framework. The Wiccan Rede encourages individuals to live authentically, embracing their desires and choices, provided they do not cause harm to themselves or others. This pursuit of personal freedom is tempered by the ethical responsibility to minimize harm and to consider the consequences of one's actions on the well-being of all living beings. While this ethical balance is not without its complexities and challenges, it remains a central and enduring principle in Wiccan spirituality. Through the ongoing exploration of this ethical dilemma, practitioners find a moral framework that empowers them to live in harmony with themselves, the natural world, and the greater cosmic order, fostering a deep sense of connection and reverence for all living beings.

Karmic Principles in Wicca

Karma, a concept originating from Hinduism and Buddhism, has found its way into various spiritual and philosophical traditions worldwide, including Wicca. Within Wicca, karma is often understood through the Law of Return and the Threefold Law, both of which emphasize the consequences of one's actions and intentions. In this section, we will explore the karmic principles in Wicca, their significance, and how they shape the ethical framework of the tradition.

The Law of Return, often called the "Law of Three" or "Law of Cause and Effect," is a central karmic principle in Wicca. It posits that whatever energy or intention a person puts out into the world will return to them threefold. In other words, the consequences of one's actions, be they positive or negative, will be magnified and reflected back upon the individual. This principle underscores the belief that actions have repercussions and that individuals are responsible for the energy they emit into the universe. The

Law of Return serves as a reminder of the interconnectedness of all life and the importance of ethical conduct. It encourages practitioners to be mindful of their actions and intentions, as they directly influence the quality of their lives. This principle aligns with the broader Wiccan belief in living in harmony with nature and recognizing the inherent wisdom of the natural world. It reinforces the idea that individuals are part of a greater cosmic web, and their actions can have far-reaching effects.

One of the key aspects of the Law of Return is the emphasis on personal responsibility. Wiccans are encouraged to consider the potential consequences of their choices, recognizing that every action, whether mundane or magical, carries an energetic imprint. This awareness cultivates mindfulness and ethical behavior, as practitioners strive to make choices that align with their values and minimize harm to themselves and others.

Critics of the Law of Return argue that it oversimplifies the complex nature of cause and effect, attributing all outcomes to a simple threefold return. They contend that the world does not always operate straightforwardly and that the law can lead to a deterministic view of karma. Some argue that life's circumstances and consequences are influenced by numerous individual and collective factors, making it challenging to predict how energy will return.

The Threefold Law is another karmic principle in Wicca, often intertwined with the Law of Return. This principle suggests that whatever energy or intention a person puts out into the world will return to them threefold. While the wording is similar to the Law of Return, the Threefold Law emphasizes the idea of "as you sow, so shall you reap," suggesting that the consequences of one's actions are directly proportional to the energy and intention behind them.

The Threefold Law reinforces the concept of personal responsibility and ethical conduct within Wicca. It highlights the importance of intentions, recognizing that the energy and intent behind an action are significant factors in determining the nature of the return. This principle encourages practitioners to be mindful of their motivations and desires, as they can influence the outcomes of their actions.

Like the Law of Return, the Threefold Law is often criticized for its perceived simplicity and deterministic implications. Critics argue that it can lead to a narrow and overly rigid view of karma, overlooking the complexities of life and the multitude of factors that contribute to the consequences of one's actions.

Despite the criticisms, the karmic principles of the Law of Return and the Threefold Law remain central and influential concepts in Wicca. They serve as moral compasses, guiding practitioners in their choices and behaviors. Moreover, they foster a sense of personal accountability, reminding individuals that their actions have repercussions for themselves and the world around them.

These karmic principles also extend beyond individual conduct to include broader social and environmental concerns. Some Wiccans interpret the principles as a call to engage in social justice and environmental activism, viewing them as a way to address systemic inequalities, advocate for environmental sustainability, and promote ethical living on a collective level. This perspective expands the application of these karmic principles to encompass personal conduct and collective responsibility for creating a more just and harmonious world.

In conclusion, the karmic principles of the Law of Return and the Threefold Law significantly shape Wicca's ethical framework. They emphasize the consequences of one's actions and intentions, encouraging personal responsibility, ethical conduct, and mindfulness. While these principles may be criticized for their simplicity, they remain enduring and meaningful in Wiccan spirituality. Through these karmic principles, practitioners find a moral framework that empowers them to live in harmony with themselves, the natural world, and the more significant cosmic order, fostering a deep sense of connection and reverence for all living beings.

CHAPTER IV

The Wiccan Rede

Understanding the Wiccan Rede

The Wiccan Rede, often considered one of the foundational ethical principles in Wicca, serves as a guiding light for practitioners of this modern pagan, nature-based religion. The Rede, encapsulated in the phrase "An it harm none, do what thou wilt," is a concise yet profound statement that lays the groundwork for ethical behavior within the tradition. In this section, we will explore the Wiccan Rede, its significance, and how it shapes the moral framework of Wicca.

At its core, the Wiccan Rede conveys the idea that individuals are free to live their lives authentically, pursuing their true desires and will, as long as their actions do not cause harm to themselves or others. This principle emphasizes personal freedom and autonomy, encouraging practitioners to embrace their true selves and make choices that align with their innermost desires. It implies that individuals can make choices that align with their higher selves and ethical values.

The phrase "do what thou wilt" does not endorse reckless or impulsive behavior. Instead, it calls for the responsible pursuit of one's true purpose and desires. It encourages individuals to consider the potential consequences of their actions, ensuring that their choices do not infringe upon the well-being of others or themselves. This aspect of the Rede underscores the belief in personal empowerment and self-realization, allowing individuals to explore and embrace their spiritual and personal paths fully.

Central to the Wiccan Rede is the concept of harmlessness. "An it harm none" serves as a crucial qualifier, reminding practitioners that ethical choices must prioritize the avoidance of harm. Harm in this context is not limited solely to physical injury but encompasses emotional, mental, and spiritual harm as well. Practitioners are encouraged to be mindful of the potential effects of their choices, recognizing that even seemingly minor actions can have far-reaching consequences.

The Wiccan Rede aligns with the broader Wiccan belief in living in harmony with nature. Wicca celebrates the interconnectedness of all life and the sacredness of the natural world. This reverence for life extends to the understanding that harm should be avoided whenever possible, as it disrupts the delicate balance of nature and the cosmic web that connects all living beings.

While the Wiccan Rede provides a clear ethical guideline, its application can be complex and nuanced. It acknowledges that ethical choices are not always black and white, and individuals may find themselves facing dilemmas that require careful consideration. This flexibility allows Wiccans to navigate complex moral situations and make choices that reflect their commitment to harmlessness and personal responsibility. Critics of the Wiccan Rede argue that it can be overly idealistic and simplistic, suggesting that it is nearly impossible to live without causing harm. They contend that intentional or unintentional harm is inherent in human existence and that striving for complete harmlessness is an unattainable goal. In response, some Wiccans interpret the Rede in a way that acknowledges the inherent challenges of avoiding all harm, emphasizing the intention to minimize harm and make amends when necessary.

The Wiccan Rede is not a rigid moral code but a principle that encourages thoughtful and responsible decision-making. It recognizes that individual circumstances and intentions shape ethical choices. Therefore, practitioners engage in ongoing ethical reflection and strive to make choices that align with their values while minimizing harm to themselves and others.

The ethical foundation of the Wiccan Rede extends beyond individual conduct to encompass broader social and environmental concerns. Some Wiccans interpret the Rede as a call to engage in social justice and activism, viewing it as a way to address systemic inequalities, advocate for environmental sustainability, and promote ethical living on a collective level. This perspective expands the Rede's application to encompass not only personal conduct but also collective responsibility for creating a more just and harmonious world.

In conclusion, the Wiccan Rede serves as the ethical cornerstone of Wicca, guiding practitioners in their moral and ethical decision-making. It embodies the belief in the interconnectedness of all life and the sacredness of nature, encouraging individuals to live in harmony with themselves, the natural world, and the greater cosmic order. While the Rede's emphasis on harmlessness is not without its complexities and challenges, it remains a central and enduring principle in Wiccan spirituality. Through the Wiccan Rede, practitioners find a moral framework that empowers them to navigate the intricate balance between personal freedom and ethical responsibility, fostering a deep sense of connection to the natural world and a commitment to a life lived with reverence and respect for all living beings.

Interpreting "An It Harm None, Do What Thou Wilt"

The phrase "An it harm none, do what thou wilt," often referred to as the Wiccan Rede, stands at the heart of Wicca's ethical framework. It encapsulates the principle that individuals are free to pursue their true desires and will, as long as their actions do not cause harm to themselves or others. While this ethical guideline may seem straightforward on the surface, its interpretation and application can be complex and nuanced. In this section, we will explore how Wiccans interpret and apply the Wiccan Rede, recognizing that it is a fundamental principle that fosters personal autonomy, ethical responsibility, and a deeper connection to the natural world.

At its core, the Wiccan Rede advocates for personal freedom and autonomy. It encourages individuals to embrace their true selves and make choices that align with their innermost desires and will. This interpretation of the Rede emphasizes self-empowerment and self-realization, allowing practitioners to explore and express their spiritual and personal paths fully. It implies that individuals can make choices that align with their higher selves and ethical values.

The phrase "do what thou wilt" does not endorse reckless or impulsive behavior. Instead, it calls for the responsible pursuit of one's true purpose and desires. It encourages individuals to consider the potential consequences of their actions, ensuring that their choices do not infringe upon the well-being of others or themselves. This aspect of the Rede underscores the belief in personal responsibility and ethical conduct.

Interpreting the concept of harmlessness is crucial in understanding the Wiccan Rede. Harm in this context is not limited solely to physical injury but encompasses emotional, mental, and spiritual harm as well. Practitioners are encouraged to be mindful of the potential effects of their choices, recognizing that even seemingly minor actions can have far-reaching consequences. This interpretation emphasizes the interconnectedness of all life and the importance of avoiding actions that disrupt the delicate balance of nature and the cosmic web that connects all living beings.

One interpretation of the Wiccan Rede posits that it sets a high standard for ethical behavior. Practitioners who adhere to this interpretation strive for complete harmlessness in all their magical and mundane actions. They believe that it is possible, though challenging, to live a life without causing harm to themselves or others. This interpretation strongly emphasizes mindfulness, intentionality, and ethical responsibility.

Critics of the Rede argue that striving for complete harmlessness is an idealistic goal, suggesting that it is nearly impossible to live without causing harm. They contend that intentional or unintentional harm is inherent in human existence and that the pursuit of complete harmlessness can lead to a rigid and overly simplistic view of ethics. In response, some Wiccans interpret the Rede in a way that acknowledges the inherent challenges of avoiding all harm. They emphasize the intention to minimize harm and make amends when necessary, recognizing that individual circumstances and intentions shape ethical choices.

The flexibility of interpretation is a hallmark of the Wiccan Rede. It acknowledges that ethical choices are not always black and white, and individuals may find themselves facing dilemmas that require careful consideration. This flexibility allows Wiccans to navigate complex moral situations and make choices that reflect their commitment to harmlessness and personal responsibility.

The ethical foundation of the Wiccan Rede extends beyond individual conduct to encompass broader social and environmental concerns. Some Wiccans interpret the Rede as a call to engage in social justice and activism, viewing it as a way to address systemic inequalities, advocate for environmental sustainability, and promote ethical living on a collective level. This perspective expands the Rede's application to encompass personal conduct and collective responsibility for creating a more just and harmonious world.

In conclusion, interpreting "An it harm none, do what thou wilt" is an ongoing and dynamic process within Wicca. It is a fundamental principle that fosters personal autonomy, ethical responsibility, and a deeper connection to the natural world. While interpretations of the Rede may vary among practitioners, it remains a central and enduring ethical guideline in Wiccan spirituality. Through the diverse interpretations of the Wiccan Rede, practitioners find a moral framework that empowers them to live in harmony with themselves, the natural world, and the greater cosmic order, fostering a deep sense of connection and reverence for all living beings.

Practical Applications in Daily Life

Wicca, as a modern pagan, nature-based religion, is not confined to rituals and ceremonies conducted within sacred circles. Its principles and ethics extend into the everyday lives of practitioners. Wiccans seek to live in harmony with the natural world and to align their actions with their spiritual beliefs. In this section, we will explore the practical applications of Wiccan principles in daily life, examining how these principles shape the behavior and mindset of Wiccans beyond the boundaries of their rituals.

The ethical guideline encapsulated in the Wiccan Rede is central to Wiccan practice: "An it harm none, do what thou wilt." This principle encourages practitioners to exercise personal freedom and autonomy while simultaneously advocating for ethical responsibility. In daily life, this translates into mindful decision-making, as individuals consider the potential consequences of their actions on themselves and others. Practitioners strive to avoid causing harm in all its forms, whether physical, emotional, or spiritual, and to make choices that align with their values.

One of the practical applications of the Wiccan Rede is in the realm of interpersonal relationships. Wiccans emphasize the importance of treating others with respect and compassion. They recognize the interconnectedness of all life and strive to build harmonious relationships with friends, family, and the broader community. This includes active listening, empathy, and conflict resolution techniques that promote understanding and healing. Wiccans seek to create a positive and nurturing social environment by applying the principles of harmlessness and ethical responsibility.

Environmental stewardship is another practical aspect of Wiccan practice. Wiccans hold a deep reverence for nature and acknowledge their role as stewards of the Earth. This reverence extends beyond rituals and into daily life. Practitioners often engage in eco-friendly practices, such as recycling, reducing waste, and conserving energy. They may also advocate for environmental causes, such as conservation efforts and sustainable living. For Wiccans, these actions are practical and deeply spiritual, reflecting their commitment to living in harmony with the natural world.

Wiccans also find practical applications for their spiritual beliefs in holistic well-being. Many practitioners incorporate herbalism, aromatherapy, and meditation into their daily routines. These practices are not only therapeutic but also deeply rooted in Wiccan spirituality. Herbal remedies, for instance, are seen as a way to harness the healing energies of nature. Meditation is a means of connecting with the divine and nurturing inner harmony. These holistic approaches to well-being align with Wiccan principles of connecting with the natural world and seeking personal growth.

The cycles of the seasons and the moon phases hold great significance in Wiccan practice. These natural rhythms are not limited to rituals but are integrated into daily life. For instance, practitioners may adjust their activities and goals to align with the energies of specific lunar phases. The seasons may inspire changes in diet, exercise, or daily routines. This attunement to nature's cycles fosters a deeper connection to the natural world and a sense of living in harmony with the Earth's rhythms.

Practical applications of Wiccan principles also extend to ethical decision-making in various aspects of life. When faced with choices related to work, finances, or personal relationships, practitioners consider whether their actions align with their ethical values and the principle of harmlessness. They strive to make choices that are in harmony with their spiritual beliefs, even in situations where ethical dilemmas may arise. This commitment to ethical living extends beyond religious rituals and influences the broader scope of their lives.

Critics of Wicca sometimes overlook the practical aspects of the religion, assuming it to be solely a system of rituals and ceremonies. However, Wicca is a holistic belief system that emphasizes the interconnectedness of all life and encourages a way of living that reflects these principles. Practical applications of Wiccan principles in daily life reinforce the tradition's central tenets: harmlessness, reverence for nature, personal growth, and ethical responsibility.

In conclusion, Wiccan principles are not confined to rituals and ceremonies but find practical applications in practitioners' daily lives. The Wiccan Rede guides decision-making, fostering ethical responsibility and harmlessness in interpersonal relationships and broader societal interactions. Environmental stewardship reflects the reverence for nature central to Wicca, and holistic well-being practices align with the belief in personal growth and connection to the natural world. By applying these principles in practical ways, Wiccans seek to live in harmony with themselves, the Earth, and the greater cosmic order, fostering a deep sense of connection and reverence for all living beings.

Controversies and Debates

Like any spiritual or religious tradition, Wicca is not immune to controversies and debates. While it is often associated with nature-based spirituality and ethical principles, it is a diverse and evolving belief system encompassing a wide range of beliefs, practices, and interpretations. In this section, we will explore some of the controversies and debates within the Wiccan community, highlighting the complexity and diversity of perspectives within this modern pagan tradition.

One of the ongoing debates in Wicca revolves around the issue of lineage and initiation. Some Wiccans emphasize the importance of lineage, tracing their spiritual heritage through specific initiatory traditions. They believe that the passing down of knowledge and practices through initiation is crucial for maintaining the authenticity of the tradition. Others, however, argue that spirituality is a personal journey and that formal initiation is not necessary to be a valid practitioner of Wicca. This debate raises questions about the role of tradition, authority, and personal experience within Wicca.

Another source of controversy in Wicca is the question of cultural appropriation. Wicca incorporates elements from various cultural and mythological sources, and some practitioners have been criticized for appropriating indigenous or non-European traditions. Critics argue that borrowing elements without proper understanding or respect for their cultural context can be disrespectful and perpetuate harmful stereotypes. In response, many Wiccans emphasize the importance of cultural sensitivity and strive to honor the origins of the practices they incorporate.

The role of gender in Wicca is another topic of debate. Traditional Wiccan practices often include gender-specific roles, such as the High Priestess and High Priest. While these roles have symbolic and ritual significance, they can be seen as reinforcing gender binaries and excluding non-binary or transgender individuals. Some practitioners advocate for more inclusive and flexible gender roles within Wicca, while others argue for preserving tradition and the symbolism associated with gender in ritual.

Ethical debates also exist within the Wiccan community. While the Wiccan Rede provides a central ethical guideline emphasizing harmlessness, interpretations of what constitutes harm can vary widely. Some Wiccans adhere to a strict interpretation, striving for complete harmlessness in all actions. Others take a more nuanced approach, recognizing that harm is not always avoidable and emphasizing the intention to minimize harm and make amends when necessary. These debates highlight the complexity of ethical decision-making within Wicca. Controversies can also arise around the commercialization and commodification of Wiccan practices. Some critics argue that the commercialization of Wicca, including the sale of books, tools, and magical items, can dilute the authenticity of the tradition and turn it into a consumerist venture. On the other hand, proponents of accessibility argue that making Wiccan resources more widely available can empower individuals to explore and connect with the tradition.

One of the most significant debates in Wicca revolves around its relationship with witchcraft and the broader pagan community. While many Wiccans identify as witches and see witchcraft as an integral part of their practice, not all witches identify as Wiccans. Some witches prefer a more eclectic or non-denominational approach to witchcraft and spirituality. These debates raise questions about the boundaries and definitions of Wicca and how they relate to the larger world of witchcraft and paganism.

Despite these controversies and debates, it is essential to recognize that diversity of thought and practice is a strength of the Wiccan community. Wicca is not a monolithic tradition but a tapestry of beliefs and perspectives that continue to evolve. These debates reflect the ongoing dialogue and exploration within the tradition, challenging practitioners to think critically about their beliefs and practices.

In conclusion, controversies and debates are a natural part of the Wiccan tradition, as in any religious or spiritual tradition. They highlight the diversity of perspectives and the dynamic nature of Wicca as a modern pagan tradition. While these debates can be contentious at times, they also provide opportunities for growth, reflection, and the evolution of Wiccan spirituality. Ultimately, the ability to engage in open dialogue and respectful discussion is a testament to the vitality and resilience of the Wiccan tradition.

CHAPTER V

Rituals and Practices

Types of Wiccan Rituals

Rituals are the cornerstone of Wiccan spirituality, providing a structured and symbolic means of connecting with the divine, the natural world, and the self. Wicca, a modern pagan, nature-based religion, offers a rich tapestry of rituals that serve various purposes, from celebrating the cycles of the moon and seasons to invoking specific deities or working magic. In this section, we will explore some of the common types of Wiccan rituals, each imbued with its unique significance and symbolism.

One of the most fundamental types of Wiccan rituals is the Sabbat, which celebrates the eight major festivals on the Wheel of the Year. These festivals mark key points in the changing seasons and agricultural cycles, such as the solstices, equinoxes, and the cross-quarter days. The Sabbats include Samhain, Yule, Imbolc, Ostara, Beltane, Litha, Lughnasadh, and Mabon. Each Sabbat has its symbolism, customs, and traditions, but they all share the common theme of honoring the cyclical nature of life, death, and rebirth. These rituals often involve feasting, dancing, and creating sacred circles to connect with the season's energies.

Another essential type of Wiccan ritual is the Esbat, which is conducted during the moon's phases. Wiccans believe that the moon's energy influences magical workings and personal growth. Esbats are often performed during the full moon, but some practitioners also conduct rituals during the new moon and other moon phases. These rituals may involve divination, meditation, spellwork, and the drawing down of the moon's energy. Esbats provide opportunities for Wiccans to attune themselves to the lunar cycles, harnessing the moon's power for magical and spiritual purposes.

Ceremonial Magic is a type of Wiccan ritual that draws from Western magical traditions and may involve the use of ceremonial tools, symbols, and invocations. Ceremonial magic rituals often aim to invoke or commune with specific deities, angels, or spiritual entities. These rituals are characterized by their structure and adherence to particular correspondences, such as colors, symbols, and planetary associations. While not all Wiccans practice ceremonial magic, it is an option for those who seek a more structured and formal approach to ritual work.

Initiation and Dedication rituals are significant rites of passage within many Wiccan traditions. Initiation marks the formal entry of an individual into a specific coven or tradition and involves the transmission of secret teachings, oaths, and responsibilities. On the other hand, dedication is a personal commitment to the Wiccan path and often precedes or follows initiation. These rituals are profoundly symbolic and serve to deepen a practitioner's connection to the tradition and its community.

Rites of Passage, such as handfastings (Wiccan weddings), baby blessings, and funerals, are essential in many Wiccan practices. Handfasting ceremonies bind couples together in sacred union, and baby blessings welcome newborns into the community. Funerals, or "crossings," are rituals that honor and guide the departed on their journey to the afterlife. These rites of passage emphasize the sacredness of life's transitions and the interconnectedness of all beings.

Spellwork is a prevalent aspect of Wiccan practice, and many rituals are devoted to casting spells for various purposes. Spellwork rituals may involve using herbs, candles, crystals, chants, and visualizations to manifest intentions. These rituals can be highly personal and tailored to the individual practitioner's needs and desires. While not all Wiccans engage in spellwork, it is a versatile and adaptable form of ritual that allows for a wide range of magical practices.

In addition to these types of rituals, Wicca also incorporates the worship of deities, which can involve invocations, offerings, and devotional acts. Wiccans often work with a pantheon of deities, including the God and Goddess, as well as various gods and goddesses from different cultures. Worship rituals aim to establish a connection with the divine, seek guidance, and express reverence for the gods and goddesses.

Divination is another form of Wiccan ritual that involves seeking guidance or insight through various tools, such as tarot cards, runes, scrying mirrors, or pendulums. These rituals are often performed during Esbats or other appropriate times, and they can help practitioners gain clarity, make decisions, or connect with their intuition.

It is essential to note that Wiccan rituals are highly adaptable and can be personalized to suit the needs and preferences of individual practitioners. While the types of rituals mentioned here are common within the tradition, there is no one-size-fits-all approach to Wiccan practice. The diversity of rituals and their flexibility are a testament to the inclusivity and creativity of Wiccan spirituality.

In conclusion, Wicca offers a rich tapestry of rituals that serve various purposes, from celebrating the cycles of the moon and seasons to invoking deities and working magic. These rituals are profoundly symbolic and provide opportunities for Wiccans to connect with the divine, the natural world, and themselves. Whether conducted in a coven or practiced as a solitary, rituals are at the heart of Wiccan spirituality, allowing practitioners to explore and deepen their connection to the sacred in diverse and meaningful ways.

Casting Circles

One of the fundamental practices in Wiccan rituals is casting circles, a sacred and symbolic act that serves as the foundation for various magical and spiritual workings. The casting of circles is an essential ritual technique that Wiccans use to create a consecrated and protected space, both physically and energetically. This section will explore the significance of casting circles in Wicca, the methods employed, and the purposes they serve within the tradition.

At its core, casting circles in Wicca is a means of establishing a sacred and liminal space that is neither fully of the mundane nor entirely of the spiritual realm. This circle acts as a barrier or boundary that separates the ordinary from the extraordinary, the profane from the sacred. Within this consecrated space, practitioners can connect with the divine, commune with deities, and work magic with a heightened sense of focus and intention. The casting of circles is typically done at the beginning of a ritual and is often accompanied by the consecration of ritual tools and the invocation of protective energies or deities. The specific methods and tools used in circle casting vary among Wiccan traditions and individual practitioners. However, some common elements and practices are widely recognized within the tradition.

Casting the Circle: Casting a circle typically begins with the practitioner walking the perimeter of the intended circle, often in a clockwise (deosil) direction. While doing so, they may use a ritual tool, such as an athame (ritual dagger), wand, or finger, to physically trace the circle's boundary in the air. This act is symbolic, representing the creation of a boundary between the mundane world and the sacred space within the circle.

Calling the Quarters: After the circle is cast, practitioners often invoke the energies or elements associated with the four cardinal directions: North, East, South, and West. These are known as the "quarters." The elements commonly related to the quarters are Earth, Air, Fire, and Water, respectively. Calling the quarters invites the energies and blessings of these elements into the sacred space, creating a balanced and harmonious environment.

Centering and Grounding: Before proceeding with other ritual activities, practitioners often take a moment to center themselves and ground their energy. This helps them connect with the circle's energies and align their intentions with the ritual's purpose. Centering and grounding may involve deep breathing, visualization, or meditation techniques.

Invoking Deities: Depending on the specific ritual and tradition, practitioners may invoke deities associated with their practice. This can involve calling upon particular gods and goddesses or invoking the God and Goddess in their generic forms, representing the divine masculine and feminine energies.

Magical Workings: With the circle cast and the energies aligned, Wiccans engage in various magical and spiritual practices, such as spellwork, divination, meditation, or communion with the divine. The circle acts as a container for these activities, amplifying their effectiveness and providing a focused and protected environment.

Releasing the Circle: After the ritual or magical working, the circle is typically released or "opened." This involves a similar process to the initial casting, where the practitioner walks the perimeter of the circle, often in a counterclockwise (widdershins) direction, and symbolically "breaks" the boundary. The energies raised within the circle are then released or grounded, and the space returns to its mundane state.

The casting of circles in Wicca serves several essential purposes within the tradition. Firstly, it provides protection and containment. The circle acts as a barrier that shields the practitioner from unwanted or negative energies and influences, ensuring that the ritual space remains pure and focused. It also contains the energies raised during magical workings, preventing them from dissipating into the surrounding environment.

Secondly, the circle creates a liminal space that bridges the mundane and the spiritual. Within the circle, practitioners can access heightened states of consciousness, commune with the divine, and work magic more effectively. It is a portal to the realms of the sacred and the unseen, enabling more profound spiritual experiences.

Thirdly, casting circles instills a sense of reverence and mindfulness. The act of creating a consecrated space encourages practitioners to approach their rituals and magical workings with intention, respect, and focus. It serves as a reminder of the sacredness of the moment and the importance of their actions within the ritual context.

Despite its significance and ubiquity in Wiccan practice, casting circles is not without its variations and debates within the tradition. Some practitioners prefer to work without circles, believing that the energies of the sacred are always present and do not require physical boundaries. Others may adapt or simplify circle-casting techniques to suit their individual needs and preferences.

In conclusion, casting circles is a fundamental and symbolic practice in Wicca, serving as a means of creating sacred space, protection, and a liminal bridge between the mundane and the spiritual. It is a technique that empowers practitioners to connect with the divine, work magic, and engage in rituals with intention and reverence. While the specific methods and tools may vary among different Wiccan traditions and individuals, the concept of circle casting remains a core element of the tradition, fostering a deeper connection to the sacred and the unseen realms.

The Tools of Wicca

Wicca, as a modern pagan, nature-based religion, encompasses a rich tapestry of rituals and practices. Central to these practices are the tools of Wicca, a set of symbolic instruments used in various rituals and magical workings. These tools hold both practical and symbolic significance within the tradition, serving as conduits for energy, objects of veneration, and aids in connecting with the divine. In this section, we will explore Wicca's key tools, symbolism, and roles in practicing this spiritual path.

One of the most iconic tools in Wicca is the athame. Traditionally, the athame is a black-handled, double-edged dagger with a sharp blade. It symbolizes the element of Air and is associated with the masculine divine principle. The athame is used for various ritual purposes, such as casting circles, directing energy, and drawing symbols in the air. Its symbolic role represents the power of the will and intention, as well as the ability to cut through illusions and barriers.

The wand is another essential tool in Wicca, symbolizing the element of Fire and the masculine principle. It is typically made of wood and may be adorned with crystals, feathers, or other symbols. The wand directs energy, invokes spirits, and consecrates sacred space. It is often associated with the God and is seen as an extension of the practitioner's will and magical power. Wands are highly personal tools, and many Wiccans create their own or choose one that resonates with their energy.

The cup or chalice represents the element of Water and the feminine divine principle within Wicca. It is a symbol of emotions, intuition, and receptivity. The cup holds water or other liquids for ritual purposes, such as libations or blessings. It is often associated with the Goddess and the sacred feminine energy. Sharing a drink from the chalice in a ritual can symbolize unity and communion with the divine.

The pentacle is a disc or plate inscribed with a five-pointed star enclosed within a circle, often featuring additional symbols or designs. It represents the element of Earth and the material plane. The pentacle serves as a symbol of protection, grounding, and manifestation. It is used to consecrate and bless objects and invoke the energies of the Earth element. The pentacle is associated with the physical world and the practical aspects of life.

The cauldron is a versatile tool that symbolizes the element of Water and the womb of the Goddess. It is often used for mixing herbs, incense, and potions. The cauldron can also serve as a vessel for scrying, a divination practice in which one gazes into the reflective surface of the cauldron to receive visions and insights. It is a tool of transformation and regeneration, symbolizing the cyclical nature of life, death, and rebirth.

The besom, or broom, is a tool with a dual symbolism. It represents the element of Air and is often associated with cleansing and purification. The besom is used to ritually sweep away negative energies or influences from a space, making it ready for magical or ritual work. It is also a symbol of fertility and the union of the God and Goddess, as it is sometimes used in wedding or handfasting ceremonies.

In addition to these primary tools, Wiccans often work with various other objects, such as crystals, candles, incense, and altar cloths, depending on their specific rituals and practices. These objects are chosen for their energetic properties and symbolism, enhancing the efficacy of magical workings and ritual ceremonies.

It is important to note that while these tools are significant within Wicca, they are not considered magical in and of themselves. Instead, they are seen as extensions of the practitioner's intention and will, serving as focal points for energy and symbolism. Many Wiccans choose to create or consecrate their tools, infusing them with their own energy and intention to establish a personal connection.

The use of these tools varies among different Wiccan traditions and individual practitioners. Some may use all the traditional tools, while others may employ only a few or none at all, depending on their specific path and preferences. What remains consistent is the recognition of these tools as symbolic aids in connecting with the divine, harnessing natural energies, and facilitating spiritual growth.

In conclusion, the tools of Wicca hold both practical and symbolic significance within the tradition. They are instruments of magic and ritual, serving as conduits for energy, objects of veneration, and aids in connecting with the divine. Each tool represents specific elements, energies, and aspects of the divine, allowing practitioners to work in harmony with the natural world and life cycles. While the use of these tools may vary among different Wiccan paths, their symbolic roles remain central to the practice of this modern pagan tradition.

Sabbats and Esbats

Wicca, a modern pagan, nature-based religion, is deeply rooted in the cycles of nature and the cosmos. The Sabbats and Esbats are two key components of Wiccan rituals and practices that revolve around these cycles. These celebrations serve as cornerstones of the Wiccan calendar, offering opportunities for spiritual connection, magical workings, and the reverence of the divine. In this section, we will explore the significance of Sabbats and Esbats in Wicca, their unique characteristics, and their roles in Wiccans' spiritual life.

Sabbats are the eight major festivals that mark the turning points of the Wheel of the Year. These festivals are intricately linked to the changing seasons and the agricultural cycles of planting, growth, harvest, and rest. The Sabbats are often celebrated in groups or covens, but solitary practitioners also observe them in their own way. Each Sabbat has its own unique symbolism, customs, and rituals, making them a diverse and vibrant aspect of Wiccan practice.

The first Sabbat on the Wiccan calendar is Samhain, which falls on October 31st. Samhain marks the end of the harvest season and the beginning of winter. It is a time when the veil between the physical and spiritual realms is believed to be at its thinnest, allowing for communication with ancestors and spirits. Samhain is a time of reflection, divination, and honoring the dead. Yule, celebrated around December 21st, marks the winter solstice, the year's longest night. It symbolizes the rebirth of the Sun God and the gradual return of light and warmth to the world. Wiccans often decorate trees with symbols of the Sun and the God, exchange gifts, and light candles to welcome the return of the sun's energy.

Imbolc, observed around February 2nd, heralds the first signs of spring. It is associated with the Celtic goddess

Brigid and the purification of the land. Imbolc is a time for new beginnings, creativity, and the planting of metaphorical seeds for future endeavors.

Ostara, celebrated around March 21st, marks the spring equinox when day and night are in balance. It symbolizes the awakening of nature, fertility, and the return of life to the Earth. Traditionally, it is a time for planting and sowing seeds and celebrating the Goddess in her maiden aspect.

Beltane, observed on May 1st, is a festival of love, fertility, and passion. It marks the height of spring and the union of the God and Goddess. Maypoles are often erected, and bonfires are lit to celebrate the vitality of nature and the blossoming of life.

Litha, celebrated around June 21st, is the summer solstice, marking the year's longest day. It represents the peak of the Sun, God's power, and the abundance of the Earth. It is a time for feasting, bonfires, and celebrating the beauty and bounty of the natural world.

Lughnasadh, observed on August 1st, marks the first harvest and the sacrifice of the God, who willingly gives of himself to sustain the land. It is a time for gratitude, sharing the fruits of labor, and reaping the rewards of hard work.

Mabon, celebrated around September 21st, is the autumn equinox, when day and night are once again in balance. It symbolizes the second harvest and the descent of the Goddess into the underworld. Mabon is a time for reflection, thanksgiving, and preparing for the winter months.
While Sabbats celebrate the solar and agricultural cycles, Esbats are rituals conducted during the moon's phases. The moon's energy is believed to influence magical workings and personal growth, and Esbats provide dedicated times for connecting with these lunar energies.

The most commonly observed Esbat is the Full Moon, a time when the moon is at its peak and its energies are most potent. Full Moon Esbats are often used for divination, spellwork, and raising energy for specific purposes.

Some Wiccans also observe New Moon Esbats, which occur when the moon is in its darkest phase. New Moons are associated with beginnings, making them ideal for setting intentions, making plans, and embarking on new projects. They are a time for introspection and planting the seeds of desire.

The Quarter Moons, also known as First Quarter and Last Quarter, fall between the New Moon and Full Moon phases and are less commonly observed in Wiccan practice. These phases are often seen as times of adjustment and balance, making them suitable for reflection, assessment, and fine-tuning of intentions and goals.

In both Sabbats and Esbats, the creation of sacred circles is a common practice. Circles serve to consecrate the ritual space, provide protection, and create a liminal environment where the mundane and the spiritual intersect. Within these circles, practitioners connect with the divine, perform magic, and seek spiritual insights.

In conclusion, Sabbats and Esbats are essential components of Wiccan spirituality, allowing practitioners to connect with nature's and the moon's cycles. Sabbats celebrate the solar and agricultural cycles, marking the changing seasons and the turning points of the Wheel of the Year. On the other hand, Esbats provide dedicated times for harnessing the energies of the moon, allowing for magical workings and personal growth. Together, these celebrations form the rhythm of the Wiccan calendar, fostering a deep connection to the natural world and the cosmic order while honoring the divine in its various aspects.

Spellwork and its Ethical Considerations

Spellwork is a central and widely recognized practice within Wicca, a modern pagan, nature-based religion. It involves using rituals, symbols, and focused intention to manifest desired outcomes, whether related to healing, protection, divination, or personal transformation. While spellwork can be a powerful tool for Wiccans to connect with the spiritual and natural forces, it also raises ethical considerations that are deeply woven into the fabric of the tradition. In this section, we will explore the nature of spellwork in Wicca, its ethical dimensions, and how Wiccans navigate the fine line between responsible magical practice and potential harm.

At its core, spellwork in Wicca is harnessing one's will, intention, and the energies of the natural world to effect change. Spells can take various forms, including candle magic, herbal magic, divination, and more. The efficacy of spellwork is believed to be influenced by factors such as timing (corresponding to moon phases or specific Sabbats), symbolism (the use of colors, crystals, herbs, and other correspondences), and the practitioner's focus and visualization.

Ethical considerations in spellwork are deeply rooted in the Wiccan Rede, a guiding principle that states, "An it harm none, do what thou wilt." This short but powerful phrase emphasizes the importance of avoiding harm in one's actions and intentions. Wiccans interpret the Rede as a call to consider the potential consequences of their magical workings and strive for harmlessness in all endeavors. This ethical framework encourages responsible and mindful spellcasting.

One of the key ethical considerations in spellwork is the concept of consent. Wiccans are taught to respect the free will and autonomy of individuals. Thus, casting spells on others without their knowledge or consent is generally seen as unethical. Love spells, in particular, are a contentious issue within Wiccan ethics. While love is a legitimate desire, manipulating someone's feelings or desires against their will is considered a violation of the Rede. Wiccans who wish to use love spells are encouraged to focus on attracting love into their own lives or strengthening existing relationships rather than attempting to control the feelings of others.

Another ethical consideration in spellwork revolves around the concept of balance and the Law of Return, often referred to as the "Threefold Law" or the "Law of Karma." This belief suggests that the energy and intentions one puts into the universe will return to them threefold, whether as blessings or consequences. This principle encourages practitioners to be mindful of the energy they release through spellwork. Using magic for destructive or harmful purposes can have repercussions on the practitioner's own life, reinforcing the importance of adhering to the Wiccan Rede's harmlessness principle.

Spellwork ethics also extend to the use of curses and hexes. While some Wiccans argue that there may be situations where defensive magic, such as protective spells or bindings, is justified, the casting of curses is generally discouraged within the tradition. Curses are seen as harmful and negative magic that can create a cycle of negativity and harm in the practitioner's life. Many Wiccans prefer to focus on protective and banishing spells as alternatives to curses, emphasizing the importance of using magic responsibly.

Ethical considerations also come into play when working with spirits, deities, or other supernatural entities in spellwork. Wiccans believe in building respectful and mutually beneficial relationships with these beings. Attempting to compel or control them through magical means is viewed as disrespectful and potentially dangerous. Instead, practitioners are encouraged to seek guidance, blessings, or partnerships through offerings, prayers, and invocations.

In practice, Wiccans often take time to reflect on their intentions and the potential consequences of their spells before casting them. They consider whether the spell aligns with harmlessness, consent, and balance principles. Some practitioners also engage in divination, such as tarot readings or pendulum dowsing, to gain insight into the likely outcomes of their magical workings.

Moreover, ethical spellwork often involves a sense of responsibility and accountability. Practitioners are encouraged to take ownership of their actions and the energy they release, whether it leads to positive or negative outcomes. This sense of responsibility extends to the care and disposal of magical tools and materials, such as candles, herbs, and crystals, which are typically handled with reverence and respect for the Earth.

In conclusion, spellwork is an integral part of Wiccan practice, offering a means of manifesting intentions and connecting with the spiritual and natural world. However, ethical considerations are deeply interwoven into the tradition, guided by the principles of the Wiccan Rede, consent, balance, and respect for the free will of others. Wiccans strive for responsible and mindful spellcasting, understanding that the energies they release through magic have the potential to shape their own lives and the world around them. In doing so, they seek to harmonize their magical practice with their ethical values and the principles of their spiritual path.

CHAPTER VI

The Inner Alchemy of Wicca

The Transformation of Self

Wicca, a modern pagan, nature-based religion, is deeply rooted in the idea of personal transformation. Central to the Wiccan path is the belief that individuals have the power to grow, evolve, and develop spiritually. This transformation of self is encouraged and celebrated within the tradition, as it leads to a deeper connection with the divine, the natural world, and one's inner potential. In this section, we will explore the concept of personal transformation in Wicca, its significance, and the methods employed by Wiccans to facilitate this journey of self- discovery and growth.

At the heart of Wiccan spirituality lies the recognition of the divine within and the interconnectedness of all things. Wiccans often refer to the phrase, "As above, so below," reflecting the belief that the macrocosm (the universe) and the microcosm (the self) are reflections of each other. This principle underscores the idea that personal transformation is attainable and essential to aligning oneself with the divine and the natural world.

Wiccan rituals and practices are designed to facilitate this transformation by providing a framework for spiritual growth and self-realization. Rituals, such as Sabbats and Esbats, offer opportunities for reflection, introspection, and communion with the divine. These sacred ceremonies help Wiccans attune themselves to the cycles of nature, the moon, and the changing seasons, fostering a deeper connection to the world around them.

Meditation is another cornerstone of personal transformation in Wicca. Through meditation, practitioners learn to quiet the mind, focus their awareness, and access deeper levels of consciousness. This practice enhances one's spiritual insight and promotes inner peace, clarity, and self-understanding. Meditation allows Wiccans to explore the depths of their own psyche, connecting with their inner wisdom and intuition.

Visualization is a powerful technique employed by Wiccans to manifest personal transformation. By using the imagination to create mental images of desired outcomes or states of being, individuals can influence their reality and shape their own destiny. Visualization is often incorporated into spellwork and other magical practices, allowing Wiccans to align their intentions with their subconscious mind and the universe's energies.

The study of symbolism and correspondences is integral to Wiccan practice and personal transformation. Wiccans work with various symbols, such as colors, elements, crystals, and herbs, to enhance their magical workings and deepen their connection to the natural and spiritual realms. Understanding the symbolism and correspondences of these elements helps practitioners align their intentions with the energies they represent, facilitating personal growth and transformation.

Shadow work is a psychological and spiritual practice that plays a significant role in the transformation of self within Wicca. It involves exploring and confronting the hidden or "shadow" aspects of one's psyche—the fears, insecurities, traumas, and unresolved issues that may hinder personal growth. Through introspection and self-acceptance, Wiccans aim to integrate these shadow aspects, allowing for healing and wholeness.

Coven and community support also contribute to personal transformation within Wicca. Many Wiccans are part of covens or spiritual communities that provide a sense of belonging, guidance, and mentorship. Within these groups, individuals can learn from experienced practitioners, share their experiences, and receive support on their spiritual journeys. The communal aspect of Wicca fosters personal growth through shared rituals, discussions, and collaborative magical workings.

Celebrating the God and Goddess, the divine masculine and feminine energies, is a core element of Wiccan practice that encourages personal transformation. Wiccans invoke and honor these deities in various forms, recognizing their presence within themselves and the world. By connecting with the God and Goddess, practitioners explore and embody both the light and shadow aspects of their own nature, fostering a sense of balance and wholeness.

Personal transformation in Wicca is not limited to the individual but extends to the world around them. Wiccans often embrace environmentalism and a deep reverence for nature, recognizing the interconnectedness of all life. By caring for the Earth and advocating for its well-being, Wiccans seek to contribute to the transformation and healing of the planet itself.

In conclusion, personal transformation is a fundamental and celebrated aspect of Wiccan spirituality. Wiccans believe in the potential for growth, self-realization, and alignment with the divine and the natural world. Through rituals, meditation, visualization, symbolism, shadow work, community support, and a reverence for nature, individuals on the Wiccan path embark on a journey of self-discovery and spiritual evolution. In doing so, they not only transform themselves but also contribute to the transformation and healing of the world around them, embodying the core principles of their spiritual tradition.

Connecting with the Divine

The profound desire to connect with the divine lies at the core of Wiccan spirituality. Wiccans view divinity as immanent, present in all aspects of existence, and accessible to those who seek it with reverence and intention. This connection with the divine is not confined to temples or formal religious institutions but is woven into the fabric of everyday life and celebrated through rituals, meditation, and a deep appreciation of nature. This section will explore the significance of connecting with the divine in Wicca, how it is practiced, and the transformative power it holds for individuals on this spiritual path.

Wiccans embrace a polytheistic or pantheistic view of divinity, recognizing many gods and goddesses or perceiving the divine as the sacred essence that infuses all living things. This diverse and flexible approach to spirituality allows individuals to connect with the divine in a way that resonates with their personal beliefs and experiences. The gods and goddesses within Wicca often represent various aspects of nature, human experience, and archetypal forces, serving as sources of inspiration, guidance, and wisdom.

Rituals are a fundamental means through which Wiccans connect with the divine. Rituals such as Sabbats (seasonal celebrations) and Esbats (moon rituals) are central to Wiccan practice. These ceremonies provide sacred spaces where practitioners can attune themselves to the rhythms of nature and the moon's cycles. Through rituals, Wiccans invoke, honor, and commune with the gods and goddesses, expressing their devotion and gratitude.

Altars play a pivotal role in Wiccan rituals and daily practice. These sacred spaces are adorned with symbolic objects, candles, incense, and representations of the deities. Altars serve as focal points for connecting with the divine, providing a physical representation of the sacred. Wiccans create a tangible connection with the gods and goddesses by tending to their altars and making offerings, deepening their spiritual bond.

Meditation is another powerful practice for connecting with the divine in Wicca. Through meditation, practitioners quiet the mind, enter a state of receptivity, and open themselves to the presence of the divine. It is a way of attuning one's consciousness to the subtle energies of the universe and allowing for direct communion with the gods and goddesses. Meditation fosters a sense of inner peace, spiritual insight, and a deepened connection to the sacred.

Nature holds a special place in Wiccan spirituality as a direct avenue for connecting with the divine. Wiccans revere the Earth as sacred and see it as a manifestation of the goddess's body. Many Wiccans find spiritual nourishment and divine connection in the natural world. They may engage in outdoor rituals, spend time in forests or by bodies of water, or simply find solace and inspiration in the beauty and cycles of nature.

Divination is a practice often employed by Wiccans to seek guidance and connect with the divine. Tools such as tarot cards, pendulums, runes, and scrying mirrors are used to tap into the wisdom of the gods and goddesses. Through divination, Wiccans gain insights, receive messages, and deepen their understanding of their spiritual path.

The concept of immanence is central to Wiccan beliefs about divinity. Wiccans see the divine as ever-present, dwelling within and around them. This perspective encourages individuals to recognize the sacred in the ordinary, infusing their daily lives with reverence and mindfulness. Simple acts like lighting a candle, tending to a garden, or sharing a meal can become sacred rituals that foster a sense of connection with the divine.

Wiccans also emphasize the idea of personal experience and revelation in their spirituality. They believe that each individual has the potential to have direct experiences of the divine and receive personal revelations. This encourages a deep sense of autonomy and empowerment, as individuals are encouraged to trust their own intuition and spiritual insights.

Furthermore, the community plays a vital role in connecting with the divine in Wicca. Many Wiccans participate in covens or spiritual groups where they come together to celebrate rituals, share experiences, and support one another on their spiritual journeys. The collective energy and shared devotion within a community can enhance the sense of divine connection and create a supportive environment for personal and spiritual growth.

In conclusion, connecting with the divine is at the heart of Wiccan spirituality. Wiccans seek to cultivate a profound and personal relationship with the gods and goddesses, drawing inspiration, guidance, and wisdom from their divine presence. Individuals on the Wiccan path nurture this sacred connection through rituals, meditation, altars, divination, and a deep reverence for nature. The belief in immanence and personal revelation empowers Wiccans to recognize the divine daily and trust their own spiritual experiences. Ultimately, the pursuit of divine connection in Wicca is a transformative journey that enriches the spiritual lives of practitioners and deepens their understanding of the sacred in all things.

Meditation and Visualization

Meditation and visualization are integral to Wiccan practice, offering pathways to profound spiritual experiences and inner transformation. Rooted in ancient traditions, these practices serve as vehicles for connecting with the divine, attuning to the rhythms of nature, and exploring the depths of one's own consciousness. In this section, we will delve into the significance of meditation and visualization within Wicca, how they are practiced, and their profound effects on Wiccans' spiritual lives.

Meditation, in its various forms, is central to Wiccan spirituality. At its core, meditation involves the intentional and focused contemplation of thoughts, images, or energies. Wiccans use meditation to quiet the mind, achieve states of deep relaxation, and enter altered states of consciousness. By doing so, they seek to connect with the divine, gain spiritual insights, and deepen their understanding of the self and the world.

One of Wicca's most common forms of meditation is guided meditation, where practitioners are led through a visualized journey or narrative by a guide or their inner voice. Guided meditations often incorporate elements of nature, myth, or spiritual symbolism, allowing individuals to explore different realms, meet spiritual beings, or experience personal transformation. These meditations serve as tools for inner exploration, spiritual growth, and communion with the divine.

Trance meditation, a deeper and more immersive form of meditation, is also practiced in Wicca. In trance meditation, individuals enter a state of altered consciousness, often accompanied by rhythmic drumming, chanting, or repetitive movements. This trance state allows for a heightened connection with the divine and a sense of direct communion with spiritual energies or entities. Trance meditation can be a profound and transformative experience, leading to deep insights and personal revelations.

Mindfulness meditation is another approach embraced by Wiccans. This form of meditation involves paying close attention to the present moment without judgment. Mindfulness meditation can be integrated into daily life, allowing individuals to develop greater awareness, focus, and presence. By practicing mindfulness, Wiccans cultivate a deep sense of connection with the natural world and the divine that permeates all things.

In addition to meditation, visualization is a potent tool Wiccans employs to manifest intentions, deepen their spiritual practice, and connect with the sacred. Visualization is the practice of creating vivid mental images in the mind's eye, often in conjunction with focused intention and ritual. Wiccans use visualization to channel their energy, direct their will, and tap into the power of the subconscious mind.

Candle magic, a form of visualization, is common in Wicca. During candle magic rituals, practitioners focus their intent and visualize their desired outcome while gazing at a lit candle. The candle's flame symbolizes transformation and illumination, and the practitioner's focused visualization imbues the candle with their intention. Lighting a candle and concentrating on its flame can create a profound sense of connection with the divine and facilitate personal transformation.

Circle casting, a foundational practice in Wiccan ritual, involves visualizing the creation of a sacred circle or sphere of energy around the ritual space. This visualization consecrates and protects the area, creating a liminal space where the mundane and the spiritual intersect. Through circle casting, Wiccans connect with the divine and create a sacred container for their magical workings and communion with the gods and goddesses.

Visualization is also an essential aspect of pathworking, a practice in which individuals visualize themselves walking specific paths or landscapes associated with the gods, goddesses, or spiritual concepts. Pathworking allows practitioners to deepen their understanding of deity, gain insights into their own psyche, and experience personal transformation. It is a means of journeying into the realm of the divine and exploring the mysteries of the spiritual world.

In conclusion, meditation and visualization are powerful tools within the Wiccan practice, facilitating inner journeys to the sacred and fostering spiritual growth. Whether through guided meditation, trance meditation, mindfulness meditation, or the practice of visualization in rituals like candle magic and circle casting, Wiccans harness the power of their minds and imagination to connect with the divine, manifest their intentions, and deepen their spiritual understanding. These practices empower individuals on the Wiccan path to explore the depths of their own consciousness, commune with the gods and goddesses, and experience personal transformation, ultimately enriching their spiritual lives and connection to the sacred.

Personal Growth and Healing

Personal growth and healing are central themes within Wiccan spirituality, reflecting the belief in the continuous evolution of the self and the capacity for inner transformation. Wicca, a modern pagan, nature-based religion, strongly emphasizes self-discovery, self-improvement, and the pursuit of balance and harmony in one's life. Through various practices, rituals, and principles, Wiccans embark on a journey of self- exploration and healing that leads to a deeper connection with the divine, the natural world, and their own inner potential. This section will explore the significance of personal growth and healing in Wicca, the methods employed for self-discovery and healing, and the transformative power of these processes.

At the heart of Wiccan spirituality lies the belief in the interconnectedness of all things, emphasizing the relationship between the self, nature, and the divine. Wiccans see themselves as integral parts of the natural world and view personal growth and healing as a means of restoring and nurturing this connection. Pursuing personal growth and healing aligns with the Wiccan Rede, which encourages practitioners to "harm none" and emphasizes ethical conduct in all aspects of life.

Rituals and ceremonies play a significant role in personal growth and healing within Wicca. Wiccans celebrate the changing seasons through Sabbats and honor the moon's phases with Esbats. These rituals provide opportunities for reflection, introspection, and spiritual communion. Through rituals, individuals can release negative energies, set intentions for personal growth, and seek healing and transformation. Participating in sacred ceremonies fosters a sense of connection with the divine and the natural world, promoting spiritual and emotional healing.

Meditation and visualization are essential practices in Wiccan spirituality that contribute to personal growth and healing. Meditation encourages individuals to quiet the mind, focus their awareness, and access deeper levels of consciousness. It promotes inner peace, clarity, and self-understanding, facilitating emotional healing and personal transformation. On the other hand, visualization allows practitioners to create mental images of desired outcomes or states of being. Through focused visualization, Wiccans can influence their reality, manifest positive changes in their lives, and embark on a path of personal growth and healing.

Shadow work is a psychological and spiritual practice that plays a significant role in personal growth and healing within Wicca. It involves exploring and confronting the hidden or "shadow" aspects of one's psyche—the fears, insecurities, traumas, and unresolved issues that may hinder personal growth and well-being. By acknowledging and integrating these shadow aspects, individuals can heal emotional wounds, develop self-acceptance, and move towards wholeness. Shadow work is a transformative process that allows Wiccans to embrace their authentic selves and foster personal growth.

Candle magic is a form of spellwork frequently used for personal growth and healing in Wicca. Through the symbolism of candles, practitioners can focus their intent, visualize their desired outcomes, and engage in the process of self-improvement and healing. For example, a green candle may be used to represent growth and abundance, while a blue candle may symbolize healing and emotional well-being. By incorporating candle magic into their rituals and spells, Wiccans work to manifest positive changes in their lives and promote their personal growth and healing.

Herbal magic and crystal healing are additional tools employed in Wiccan practice for personal growth and healing. Wiccans believe that herbs and crystals possess specific energies and properties that can aid in physical, emotional, and spiritual healing. By working with these natural elements, practitioners can enhance their personal growth journey and address various aspects of their well-being. For example, lavender may be used for relaxation and stress relief, while amethyst crystals are associated with spiritual growth and clarity of mind.

Community support is another significant aspect of personal growth and healing in Wicca. Many Wiccans belong to covens or spiritual communities where they find a sense of belonging, guidance, and mentorship. Within these groups, individuals can share their experiences, receive support on their spiritual journeys, and engage in collective healing rituals. The communal aspect of Wicca provides a supportive environment for personal growth and healing, fostering a sense of connection and shared purpose.

In conclusion, personal growth and healing are intrinsic to Wiccan spirituality, reflecting the belief in the continuous evolution of the self and the interconnectedness of all things. Through rituals, meditation, visualization, shadow work, candle magic, herbal magic, crystal healing, and community support, Wiccans embark on a journey of self-discovery and healing that deepens their connection with the divine, the natural world, and their own inner potential. This transformative process enables individuals to address emotional wounds, foster self-acceptance, and manifest positive changes in their lives, ultimately leading to personal growth and a harmonious relationship with the sacred and the world around them.

CHAPTER VII

Wicca and Nature

Nature as Sacred

In the heart of Wiccan spirituality lies a profound reverence for the natural world—recognizing nature as sacred, divine, and intimately interconnected with the human experience. Wicca, a modern pagan, nature-based religion, celebrates the Earth as a living, sacred entity, and views all of existence as interconnected and imbued with spiritual significance. This deep connection to nature is not merely a philosophical belief but woven into the fabric of Wiccan practice and rituals. In this section, we will explore the significance of nature as sacred within Wicca, how it is honored and celebrated, and the transformative power it holds for Wiccans on their spiritual journey.

Wiccans embrace a pantheistic or panentheistic perspective, perceiving the divine as immanent in all aspects of existence. Nature, for Wiccans, is not a separate or distant entity but is seen as the embodiment of the divine—the living body of the Earth Goddess and the vital energy of the God. This perspective fosters a deep sense of reverence for the natural world and all its manifestations.

Rituals and ceremonies are integral to Wiccan practice and provide opportunities for Wiccans to honor and connect with the sacredness of nature. Wiccans celebrate the changing seasons through Sabbats and the phases of the moon through Esbats, aligning their spiritual lives with the natural cycles. These rituals are often conducted outdoors, allowing practitioners to immerse themselves in nature's beauty and to connect with the elemental forces that shape the Earth.

Circle casting is a foundational practice in Wiccan ritual, involving the creation of a sacred circle that represents the boundary·between the mundane and the spiritual realms. The act of casting a circle not only consecrates the ritual space but also serves as an acknowledgment of the sacredness of nature. It marks the area as a liminal space where the divine is honored, and where Wiccans can commune with the land's elements and spirits.

Altars are another vital aspect of Wiccan practice that reflect the sacredness of nature. Adorned with symbols of the elements, representations of the God and Goddess, and offerings of fruits, flowers, and herbs, altars serve as focal points for connecting with the divine. Through the arrangement of these sacred items, Wiccans express their reverence for nature and their recognition of its significance in their spiritual journey.

Nature walks and meditation in natural settings are practices cherished by Wiccans to deepen their connection with the Earth as sacred. Spending time in forests, by rivers, or in meadows allows practitioners to attune themselves to the rhythms of nature and the energies of the land. Through mindfulness and contemplation in these natural settings, Wiccans experience a sense of communion with the Earth and a deepening of their spiritual connection.

Wiccans also engage in environmental activism and stewardship as an expression of their reverence for nature as sacred. Many Wiccans advocate for the protection of the environment, the conservation of natural resources, and the promotion of sustainable practices. This commitment to ecological responsibility stems from the belief that the Earth is not merely a resource to be exploited but a living being deserving of respect and care.

Herbalism and crystal work are practices within Wicca that draw on the sacred properties of plants and minerals. Wiccans believe that herbs and crystals possess specific energies and healing properties. By working with these natural elements, practitioners deepen their connection to the Earth and seek to align themselves with its wisdom and vitality. These practices serve as a tangible way to honor and celebrate the sacredness of nature.

Animal symbolism and totemism are also prevalent within Wiccan spirituality. Wiccans often connect with the spirits of animals and incorporate their symbolism into their practice. By recognizing the significance of animals in their lives and rituals, practitioners embrace the interconnectedness of all living beings and celebrate the diversity and wisdom of the natural world.

In conclusion, nature as sacred is at the core of Wiccan spirituality—a belief that the Earth is a living, divine entity intimately connected with the human experience. Through rituals, circle casting, altars, nature walks, meditation, environmental activism, herbalism, crystal work, and animal symbolism, Wiccans express their reverence for the natural world and their desire to align themselves with its wisdom and vitality. This profound connection to nature serves as a source of inspiration, guidance, and spiritual nourishment, enriching the lives of Wiccans and deepening their understanding of the sacred in all things. It is a testament to the enduring bond between humanity and the Earth—a bond that Wiccans hold sacred and celebrate in their spiritual journey.

Ecological Responsibility

Ecological responsibility is a foundational principle within Wiccan spirituality, reflecting a deep reverence for the natural world and a commitment to safeguarding the Earth as a sacred and interconnected entity. Wicca, a modern pagan, nature-based religion, views the environment as a living manifestation of the divine and acknowledges the intricate web of life that sustains all beings. This perspective fosters a profound sense of ecological responsibility among Wiccans, who strive to live in harmony with nature, promote environmental stewardship, and advocate for sustainable practices. This section will explore the significance of ecological responsibility within Wicca, the practices employed to honor the Earth, and the transformative power it holds for individuals and the broader community.

Central to Wiccan spirituality is the belief in the interconnectedness of all things, emphasizing the relationship between humanity, the natural world, and the divine. Wiccans recognize the Earth as a sacred and sentient being, often personified as the Earth Goddess, and they view themselves as integral parts of the web of life. This perspective underscores the importance of ecological responsibility as a moral and spiritual imperative.

Rituals and ceremonies within Wicca provide dedicated moments for practitioners to express their ecological responsibility. Wiccans celebrate the changing seasons through Sabbats and honor the moon's phases through Esbats, aligning their spiritual lives with the cycles of nature. These rituals serve as reminders of the sacredness of the Earth and reinforce the connection between the divine and the natural world. Through these ceremonies, Wiccans express gratitude for the gifts of the Earth and renew their commitment to ecological responsibility.

Circle casting, a foundational practice in Wiccan ritual, not only creates a sacred space but also reinforces the sacredness of the Earth. When practitioners cast a circle, they mark the area as a liminal space where the mundane and the spiritual intersect. This act acknowledges the Earth as a living entity and serves as a reminder of the sanctity of the land upon which the circle is cast. It reinforces the idea that ecological responsibility is woven into the very fabric of Wiccan practice.

Altars are another means through which Wiccans express their ecological responsibility. Adorned with symbols of the elements, representations of the God and Goddess, and offerings of fruits, flowers, and herbs, altars serve as focal points for connecting with the divine and the Earth. By arranging these sacred items, practitioners express their reverence for the natural world and their commitment to ecological responsibility. The act of tending to the altar embodies their devotion to the Earth.

Wiccans also engage in environmental activism as an expression of their ecological responsibility. Many Wiccans are passionate advocates for the protection of the environment, the conservation of natural resources, and the promotion of sustainable practices. Their activism may take various forms, such as participating in conservation efforts, supporting eco-friendly initiatives, or advocating for policies prioritizing the planet's well-being. This activism reflects a commitment to ecological responsibility that extends beyond spiritual practice and into the realm of social and environmental action.

Herbalism and crystal work, two practices within Wicca, emphasize the interconnectedness between humans and the natural world. Wiccans believe that herbs and crystals possess specific energies and properties that can be harnessed for various purposes, including healing and spiritual growth. Through these practices, practitioners deepen their connection to the Earth and seek to align themselves with its wisdom and vitality. This fosters an intimate relationship with the environment and reinforces the importance of ecological responsibility.

Wiccans also embrace sustainable living as a practical expression of their ecological responsibility. Many practitioners strive to reduce their ecological footprint by adopting eco-friendly habits, such as conserving energy, minimizing waste, supporting local and organic agriculture, and reducing their consumption of resources. Sustainable living aligns with the Wiccan principles of balance and harmony with nature, reflecting a commitment to reducing harm to the Earth.

In conclusion, ecological responsibility is Wiccan spirituality's fundamental and deeply cherished principle. Wiccans view the Earth as a sacred and interconnected entity, and they express their reverence for the natural world through rituals, altars, activism, herbalism, crystal work, and sustainable living practices. This commitment to ecological responsibility is not merely a moral imperative but also a spiritual one—a reflection of the belief in the interconnectedness of all things and the responsibility to care for the Earth as a living manifestation of the divine. Through these practices, Wiccans contribute to the planet's well-being and foster a deep sense of harmony with the sacred Earth they hold dear.

Herbalism and Wicca

Herbalism is an ancient practice with a special place within Wicca, a modern pagan, nature-based religion. For Wiccans, herbs are deeply intertwined with their spiritual beliefs and reverence for the natural world. Herbs are seen as more than mere botanical entities; they are regarded as living manifestations of the Earth's energy, embodying nature's wisdom and healing properties. This sacred connection to herbs and their use in both spiritual and practical contexts is a cornerstone of Wiccan practice. In this section, we will explore the significance of herbalism within Wicca, how herbs are employed in rituals and spellwork, and the deep-rooted connection between herbalism and the Wiccan worldview.

At the heart of Wiccan spirituality is the belief in the interconnectedness of all things, emphasizing the relationship between humanity, the natural world, and the divine. Wiccans see themselves as integral parts of the web of life and view herbs as living expressions of the Earth's energy and vitality. This perspective fosters a profound reverence for plants' healing and magical properties, recognizing them as sacred gifts from the Earth Goddess.

Herbs in rituals and ceremonies are a common feature of Wiccan practice. Wiccans celebrate the changing seasons through Sabbats and honor the moon's phases through Esbats, aligning their spiritual lives with the cycles of nature. Herbs play a central role in these rituals, symbolizing the energies of the season or the practitioner's intentions. For example, herbs associated with growth and renewal, such as rosemary and lavender, may be used to bless the circle and participants during the spring Sabbat of Ostara. Incorporating herbs into rituals serves as a way to attune with nature's rhythms and draw on the plant's energies for magical and spiritual purposes.

Herbal correspondences are fundamental to the use of herbs in Wiccan spellwork and rituals. Each herb is believed to possess specific energies, correspondences, and magical properties that suit particular intentions. Wiccans meticulously select herbs that align with their goals, whether it be for protection, healing, love, or divination. For instance, rosemary is associated with protection and memory enhancement, while lavender is renowned for its calming and purifying properties. The careful choice of herbs reflects a deep understanding of the interconnectedness of herbs and their relationship to the universe's energies.

Herbal magic, a form of spellwork, is common in Wicca. Wiccans prepare and consecrate herbal charms, sachets, potions, and teas to harness the energies of herbs for magical purposes. The act of crafting and working with herbs in this way is seen as a collaboration with the Earth's wisdom and a means of channeling divine energy. For example, an herbal sachet containing rose petals, lavender, and chamomile might be used to attract love and promote emotional healing. The potency of herbal magic lies not only in the herbs themselves but in the intention and energy infused by the practitioner.

Herbal remedies in Wicca extend beyond magical applications; they also encompass healing and wellness. Many Wiccans are drawn to the holistic and natural aspects of herbal medicine. Herbal remedies may be used to address physical ailments, boost emotional well-being, or enhance spiritual practices. Herbs such as echinacea, calendula, and sage are valued for their medicinal properties, and Wiccans often incorporate them into their daily lives to promote health and vitality.

Herb gardens are common features in the homes of many Wiccans, serving as both practical resources and sacred spaces. These gardens are carefully tended and often include a variety of herbs with magical and healing properties. Tending to an herb garden is not only a practical endeavor but also a spiritual one, fostering a deeper connection with the Earth and the energies of the plants. It allows practitioners to harvest herbs for both magical and medicinal purposes, reinforcing the sacred bond between humanity and nature.

In conclusion, herbalism occupies a significant and sacred place within Wicca, reflecting Wiccans' deep reverence for the natural world and the interconnectedness of all life. Herbs are cherished for their healing properties, magical correspondences, and their role in rituals and ceremonies. The use of herbs in Wicca is not merely a practical or magical endeavor but a spiritual one that embodies the belief in the sacredness of the Earth and the wisdom of nature. Through herbalism, Wiccans connect with the energies of the Earth Goddess, draw on the healing powers of plants, and deepen their understanding of the sacred relationship between humanity and the natural world.

Animal Totems and Spirit Guides

In the realm of Wicca, a modern pagan, nature-based religion, the natural world is regarded as a source of profound wisdom, inspiration, and guidance. Among the various facets of nature, animals hold a special place as messengers of the divine and as guides on the spiritual journey. Wiccans believe that animals possess unique qualities and energies that can provide insight into their own lives and offer spiritual guidance. This belief has led to the practice of working with animal totems and spirit guides—a connection to the animal kingdom that has deepened their understanding of the natural world and enriched their spiritual lives. In this section, we will explore the significance of animal totems and spirit guides within Wicca, how they are encountered and honored, and the transformative power they hold for practitioners.

At the heart of Wiccan spirituality lies the belief in the interconnectedness of all things, emphasizing the relationship between humanity, the natural world, and the divine. Wiccans perceive animals as vital components of this intricate web of life, and they recognize that animals possess unique qualities, behaviors, and symbolism that can provide spiritual insights. This perspective fosters a profound reverence for the animal kingdom and the belief that animals can serve as spiritual allies and guides. Animal totems, also known as power animals or animal guides, are spiritual allies that are believed to be linked to individuals throughout their lives. Wiccans may encounter their animal totem through dreams, visions, meditation, or a deep affinity for a particular animal.

These totems are seen as sources of guidance, protection, and wisdom. For example, a person with a wolf totem may be drawn to the wolf's qualities of loyalty, intuition, and a strong sense of community. The wolf becomes a symbol of strength and guidance on their spiritual journey.

Spirit guides, on the other hand, are often considered to be specific animals or spiritual beings that offer guidance during particular phases of one's life or on specific aspects of their path. These guides may come and go as needed, offering their wisdom and support when the time is right. Spirit guides can be encountered in meditation, dreams, or through synchronicities in the physical world. They are viewed as allies who offer insights and assistance on the practitioner's journey.

The process of connecting with animal totems and spirit guides is highly personal and often involves meditation, visualization, and inner reflection. Many Wiccans engage in guided meditations to meet their totem animals or spirit guides. During these meditations, they enter a relaxed state of consciousness and journey inward to meet the animal or guide. Visualization is crucial as practitioners often describe encountering their totems or guides in a natural setting, such as a forest, cave, or meadow. These encounters serve as profound experiences of connection with the natural world and are believed to provide guidance and wisdom.

Animal symbolism is prevalent within Wiccan rituals, spellwork, and divination. Wiccans often call upon the energies and symbolism of animals to enhance their magical practices. For example, invoking the owl's spirit may be done to seek wisdom, while invoking the energy of the hawk may aid in gaining a broader perspective or clarity. In divination, the appearance or behavior of animals is often interpreted as messages from the divine or as signs of guidance and insight.

Animal offerings are another way in which Wiccans honor and connect with animal totems and spirit guides. Offerings can include food, herbs, or other items associated with the animal. These offerings are made as tokens of gratitude and respect for the guidance and wisdom provided by the animals. Such offerings reflect the belief in the reciprocal relationship between humans and the natural world.

In conclusion, animal totems and spirit guides are integral aspects of Wiccan spirituality, serving as messengers of the divine and as guides on the spiritual journey. Wiccans believe that animals possess unique qualities and energies that offer insights and wisdom for their lives. Through meditation, visualization, animal symbolism, and offerings, practitioners deepen their connection to the animal kingdom, drawing upon the spiritual allies and guides that share their path. This profound connection to the natural world enriches the spiritual lives of Wiccans, deepens their understanding of the interconnectedness of all life, and offers a source of guidance and inspiration on their spiritual journey.

CHAPTER VIII

Wicca in Modern Society

Wicca's Place in Contemporary Spirituality

In the diverse landscape of contemporary spirituality, Wicca stands out as a modern pagan religion deeply rooted in nature and ancient traditions. Emerging in the mid-20th century, Wicca has grown and evolved, attracting a diverse community of practitioners who find meaning, connection, and spirituality in its practices. While often misunderstood or misrepresented in popular culture, Wicca has seen its place as a valid and vibrant path within the broader tapestry of contemporary spirituality. In this section, we will explore Wicca's place in contemporary spirituality, its core beliefs and practices, its appeal to modern seekers, and its contributions to the ever-evolving spiritual landscape.

At its core, Wicca is a nature-based, polytheistic religion that reveres the Earth and views it as sacred. Central to Wiccan spirituality is the belief in the interconnectedness of all things, emphasizing the relationship between humanity, the natural world, and the divine. Wiccans see themselves as stewards of the Earth, drawing inspiration from the cycles of nature and the wisdom of ancient pagan traditions. This deep connection to nature sets Wicca apart as a spiritual path that encourages environmental stewardship and celebrates the Earth's sacredness.

Rituals and ceremonies play a significant role in Wiccan practice and are often conducted outdoors to immerse practitioners in the natural world. Wiccans celebrate the changing seasons through Sabbats and honor the moon's phases through Esbats, aligning their spiritual lives with the cycles of nature. These rituals provide moments of reflection, gratitude, and connection with the divine. Through ceremonial practices, Wiccans seek to attune with the energies of the Earth, fostering a sense of harmony and balance in their lives.

Wicca is a religion that celebrates diversity and inclusivity within its community. Unlike other religious traditions, Wicca does not impose a single dogma or set of beliefs but encourages individuals to explore and develop their spirituality. This openness to diverse perspectives and practices has attracted people from various backgrounds and belief systems, making Wicca an inclusive and welcoming path for seekers who resonate with its core values.

The concept of witchcraft is central to Wiccan practice, and many Wiccans identify as witches. Witchcraft, in the context of Wicca, is not about wielding supernatural powers or causing harm but is a spiritual practice rooted in connecting with the natural world and harnessing its energies for personal growth, healing, and transformation. Wiccans often engage in spellwork, which involves the use of symbolism, visualization, and natural elements like herbs and crystals to manifest positive changes in their lives. This aspect of Wiccan practice has resonated with those seeking a hands-on and empowering form of spirituality.

Female empowerment and the veneration of the Goddess are significant aspects of Wiccan spirituality. Wicca acknowledges the divine feminine in the form of the Goddess, representing aspects of fertility, nurturing, and wisdom. This emphasis on the feminine principle has attracted individuals seeking a spiritual path that honors and empowers women, promoting gender equality and self-empowerment.

Wicca's place in contemporary spirituality extends beyond its rituals and practices. It has found a home in the digital age, with many online resources, communities, and educational platforms dedicated to the study and practice of Wicca. The internet has allowed practitioners to connect, share knowledge, and seek guidance from experienced Wiccans, fostering a global community of like-minded individuals.

Wicca has also made contributions to the broader dialogue on spirituality and ethics. The ethical foundation of Wicca, encapsulated in the Wiccan Rede ("An it harm none, do what thou wilt"), emphasizes personal responsibility and ethical conduct in all aspects of life. This principle encourages practitioners to consider the consequences of their actions and strive for harmlessness. In a world grappling with ethical dilemmas, environmental concerns, and questions of personal responsibility, Wicca's emphasis on ethics and interconnectedness offers valuable insights and perspectives.

In conclusion, Wicca's place in contemporary spirituality is characterized by its nature-based spirituality, inclusivity, and emphasis on personal empowerment and ethical conduct. It has evolved from its roots in the mid-20th century to become a vibrant and diverse spiritual path that resonates with modern seekers. As individuals continue to seek meaningful connections with the Earth, the divine, and their own inner selves, Wicca's emphasis on interconnectedness, reverence for nature, and empowerment continues to offer a relevant and enriching spiritual journey in the ever-evolving landscape of contemporary spirituality.

Challenges and Misconceptions

Wicca, a modern pagan, nature-based religion, has often been shrouded in mystery, misconception, and prejudice.

Despite its growth and acceptance in contemporary society, challenges and misconceptions persist, stemming from a lack of knowledge and misunderstandings perpetuated by popular culture and historical biases. In this section, we will explore some of Wiccans' challenges and the misconceptions surrounding their faith, shedding light on the realities of this diverse and vibrant spiritual path.

One of the most significant challenges for Wiccans is misunderstanding and prejudice. Throughout history, paganism and witchcraft have been subject to persecution and demonization, leading to deeply ingrained biases. These biases continue to manifest as discrimination, fear, and mistrust towards Wiccans. Many misconceptions about Wicca are rooted in this historical context. Wiccans are often wrongly associated with Satanism, dark magic, or malevolent intentions, when, in fact, their beliefs center on nature worship, ethical principles, and personal growth.

Secrecy and privacy are essential aspects of Wiccan practice, and this can contribute to misunderstandings. Wiccans often choose to keep their faith private due to concerns about discrimination or misunderstanding from family, friends, or the broader community. This secrecy can sometimes be misconstrued as a sinister or secretive agenda when, in reality, it is a personal choice made to protect one's spiritual path.

Another challenge facing Wiccans is cultural appropriation. In an age of increased awareness about the importance of respecting indigenous and marginalized cultures, some individuals within the broader pagan community, including Wicca, have been criticized for appropriating elements of other cultures without proper understanding or respect. Like practitioners of different spiritual paths, Wiccans must navigate the complex terrain of cultural sensitivity and authenticity, striving to avoid appropriation while honoring their own spiritual journey.

Media portrayals of Wicca often perpetuate misconceptions. Television shows, movies, and books frequently depict Wicca and witchcraft in sensationalized or inaccurate ways, emphasizing stereotypes and misconceptions for entertainment value. These portrayals contribute to the misunderstanding of Wicca and can create unrealistic expectations or fears among those unfamiliar with the faith.

Misconceptions about Wicca can also arise within the broader pagan community. Some pagans hold biases against Wicca due to differences in beliefs or practices. These internal divisions can hinder solidarity and cooperation among pagan groups, preventing the exchange of knowledge and shared experiences that could benefit the entire community.

Lack of recognition is another challenge faced by Wiccans. In some countries, Wicca is not officially recognized as a religion, which can result in legal and societal challenges. Wiccans may encounter difficulties in obtaining recognition for their faith in official documents or when seeking accommodation for religious practices in various settings.

Education and outreach efforts by Wiccans and pagan organizations aim to address these challenges and dispel misconceptions. Many Wiccans actively engage in interfaith dialogue to foster understanding and tolerance among different religious communities. Educational resources, such as books, websites, and workshops, seek to provide accurate information about Wicca, its beliefs, and practices, and to counteract the perpetuation of myths and stereotypes.

Community involvement is another way in which Wiccans combat misunderstandings. By participating in community service, environmental initiatives, and charitable activities, Wiccans demonstrate their commitment to ethical principles and their desire to contribute positively to society.

In conclusion, like many spiritual paths, Wicca faces challenges and misconceptions that stem from historical biases, popular culture, and a lack of understanding. Discrimination, secrecy, cultural appropriation, media portrayals, internal divisions, and lack of recognition are some of the obstacles that Wiccans encounter on their spiritual journey. However, Wiccans continue to engage in education, outreach, and community involvement to dispel misconceptions, promote tolerance, and foster a greater understanding of their faith. In a world that increasingly values diversity and respect for different spiritual paths, the challenges and misconceptions faced by Wiccans serve as a reminder of the ongoing need for open dialogue, education, and acceptance within the broader spiritual and religious landscape.

Legal and Social Aspects

As Wicca has gained recognition and adherents, it has encountered a range of legal and social aspects that reflect the changing dynamics of contemporary society. These aspects encompass issues related to religious freedom, discrimination, and the broader social perception of Wicca as a modern pagan faith. In this section, we will explore Wicca's legal and social dimensions, examining the challenges and opportunities that Wiccans face in navigating a diverse and evolving cultural landscape.

One of the key legal aspects that Wiccans confront is religious freedom. In many countries, including the United States, legal protections for religious freedom are enshrined in the constitution. Like practitioners of other faiths, Wiccans have the right to practice their religion freely and without discrimination. However, the recognition of Wicca as a legitimate religion has varied, leading to legal challenges in some instances. Wiccans may encounter difficulties in securing accommodations for their religious practices, such as access to sacred spaces for rituals, time off for holidays, or the right to wear religious attire.

Discrimination and prejudice are social aspects that can impact the lives of Wiccans. Misunderstandings and stereotypes about Wicca, perpetuated by popular culture and historical biases, can lead to discrimination in various spheres of life. Wiccans may face discrimination in the workplace, in their communities, or within their own families. Fear and misunderstanding of Wicca can result in social isolation and even harassment. Education and outreach efforts within the Wiccan community aim to counteract these challenges and promote understanding. Community building is a vital social aspect of Wicca. Wiccans often come together in covens or circles to practice their faith collectively. These communities provide support, camaraderie, and spiritual guidance. However, they can also face challenges related to inclusivity and diversity. Ensuring that Wiccan communities are welcoming and respectful of individuals from various backgrounds and belief systems is an ongoing endeavor. Some Wiccans are drawn to solitary practice, while others actively seek out like-minded individuals to form spiritual communities.

Legal recognition of Wicca as a religion is another aspect that varies by country. In the United States, Wicca is generally considered a legitimate religion under the law, with practitioners afforded the same legal protections as adherents of more mainstream faiths. However, in some countries, Wicca may not receive the same level of recognition or protection, which can lead to legal and social challenges for practitioners. Obtaining recognition and rights for Wicca as a religion is an ongoing effort in some regions.

Interfaith dialogue is valuable to Wiccan engagement with the broader religious community. Many Wiccans actively participate in interfaith discussions and initiatives to foster understanding and cooperation among different religious groups. These efforts promote tolerance and respect for diverse faiths and dispel misconceptions about Wicca.

Environmental activism is a social aspect closely aligned with Wiccan spirituality. Many Wiccans view themselves as stewards of the Earth and actively engage in environmental initiatives and conservation efforts. This commitment to ecological responsibility reflects the core belief in the interconnectedness of all things and the sacredness of the natural world. Wiccans often advocate for sustainable practices and the protection of the environment, contributing to broader social discussions on environmental ethics.

In conclusion, Wicca navigates a complex landscape of legal and social aspects in contemporary society. While legal protections for religious freedom are generally in place, the recognition and accommodation of Wicca as a legitimate religion can vary by region. Discrimination, prejudice, and misunderstandings persist in some quarters, highlighting the importance of education and outreach efforts. Building inclusive and diverse communities, participating in interfaith dialogue, and advocating for environmental responsibility are all aspects of Wiccan engagement with the broader society. As Wicca continues to evolve and gain recognition, these legal and social dimensions will shape the experiences of practitioners and contribute to the ongoing dialogue on religious diversity and freedom in the modern world.

Interfaith Dialogue and Acceptance

Interfaith dialogue and acceptance hold a unique place within the practice of Wicca, a modern pagan, nature-based religion. Wiccans, who revere the interconnectedness of all things and the sacredness of the Earth, understand the importance of fostering understanding and cooperation among diverse religious traditions. This section will explore how Wicca approaches interfaith dialogue and acceptance, the significance of these aspects within the faith, and their role in promoting harmony and tolerance in a world of religious diversity.

Wicca is a religion deeply rooted in nature worship and the celebration of the cycles of life. Central to Wiccan belief is the recognition that all living beings are interconnected, and this perspective extends to the realm of interfaith dialogue. Wiccans view interfaith dialogue as a means to deepen their understanding of the diversity of spiritual paths and connect with others who are committed to spirituality and the environment.

Inclusivity and diversity are fundamental principles within Wicca, and they apply to both the Wiccan community and the broader interfaith context. Wicca encourages individuals to explore and develop their personal spiritual paths, emphasizing the value of diverse perspectives and practices. This inclusivity extends to interfaith dialogue, where Wiccans embrace opportunities to engage with individuals and groups from various religious backgrounds.

Respect for other faiths is key to interfaith dialogue and acceptance within Wicca. Wiccans understand that each religious tradition has its unique beliefs, practices, and values, and they approach interfaith conversations with an open heart and a willingness to learn. This respect is rooted in the belief that all spiritual paths hold intrinsic value and contribute to the tapestry of human understanding of the divine.

Shared values and common goals often emerge in surprising ways during interfaith dialogue. Wiccans find that, despite theological differences, there are often shared concerns and commitments among individuals from different religious traditions. Issues such as environmental stewardship, social justice, and ethical conduct frequently transcend religious boundaries. These shared values become bridges for cooperation and collaboration, fostering a sense of unity and purpose among diverse faith communities.

Interfaith initiatives and gatherings allow Wiccans to engage in meaningful dialogue and build relationships with individuals from other faiths. These initiatives may take the form of interfaith prayer services, discussion groups, workshops, or collaborative community projects. Wiccans often participate actively in such events, contributing their unique perspective on spirituality, nature, and ethics.

Promoting tolerance and understanding is a shared goal of interfaith dialogue within Wicca. Wiccans recognize that misunderstandings and prejudices about their own faith persist, much like they do for other non-mainstream spiritual paths. By engaging in open and respectful conversations, Wiccans aim to dispel misconceptions and foster tolerance for their beliefs and all faiths.

Interfaith cooperation for social and environmental causes is a natural extension of Wicca's commitment to environmental responsibility and social justice. Wiccans often collaborate with individuals and groups from different faith traditions to address pressing global issues, such as climate change, poverty, and human rights. These collaborative efforts demonstrate the practical impact of interfaith dialogue and acceptance, highlighting how diverse religious communities can work together for the betterment of society and the planet.

In conclusion, interfaith dialogue and acceptance are integral aspects of Wicca, reflecting the faith's commitment to inclusivity, respect, and cooperation with individuals from diverse religious backgrounds. Wiccans recognize the interconnectedness of all living beings and the value of diverse perspectives in understanding the sacredness of the Earth. Through interfaith dialogue, Wiccans aim to foster understanding, promote tolerance, and build bridges of cooperation with other faith traditions. In a world characterized by religious diversity, these efforts serve as a testament to the potential for harmony and unity among individuals and communities of different beliefs and practices.

CHAPTER IX

Ethics and Relationships

Love and Sexuality in Wicca

Love and sexuality are central aspects of the human experience, and they hold a unique place within the framework of Wicca, a modern pagan, nature-based religion. Wicca recognizes the profound connection between the physical, emotional, and spiritual dimensions of love and sexuality, celebrating them as sacred expressions of life's energies. In this section, we will explore how Wicca views love and sexuality, the significance of these aspects in Wiccan practice, and the principles that guide a balanced and ethical approach to love and sexuality within the faith.

Wicca is a religion that reveres the natural world and embraces the interconnectedness of all things. Within this spiritual framework, love and sexuality are seen as expressions of the divine and natural forces. Wiccans believe that the physical and the spiritual are intertwined, and they celebrate the idea that the pursuit of love and the expression of sexuality can be spiritual acts that deepen their connection to the divine and the universe.

The Goddess and the God, central figures in Wiccan theology, embody the divine feminine and masculine energies, respectively. They are often seen as lovers, symbolizing the union of opposites and the balance of complementary forces. The moon cycle, which is revered in Wicca, is often associated with the phases of the Goddess and the cycles of life, including love and fertility. Wiccans recognize that love and sexuality are a part of the natural order and celebrate them as sacred aspects of human existence.

Wiccans believe in the Great Rite, a symbolic and ritualized representation of the union between the Goddess and the God. This ritual is often performed in the form of the ritual sexual act, where the High Priest and High Priestess come together to celebrate the divine union. However, it is important to note that the ritual sexual act does not necessarily involve sexual intercourse; it can be a symbolic or metaphorical act, depending on the tradition and the preferences of the participants. The Great Rite is a powerful representation of the sacredness of love and sexuality within Wiccan practice.

Ethical principles guide the expression of love and sexuality in Wicca. One of Wicca's most well-known ethical guidelines is the Wiccan Rede, which states, "An it harm none, do what thou wilt." This principle emphasizes personal responsibility and ethical conduct in all aspects of life, including love and sexuality. Wiccans believe that love and sexual relationships should be consensual, respectful, and free from harm to all parties involved. Consent and communication are highly valued, and any form of sexual misconduct or harm is strongly discouraged within the faith.

Fertility and creativity are also associated with love and sexuality in Wicca. The act of creating life, whether in the physical sense through childbirth or in the metaphorical sense through creative endeavors, is seen as a sacred expression of love and sexuality. Wiccans often celebrate the cycles of life, death, and rebirth, which are reflected in nature and in the symbolic union of the Goddess and the God.

Gender equality is a fundamental principle in Wicca, and it extends to the realm of love and sexuality. Wiccans embrace the divine feminine and masculine energies equally, recognizing that both genders have essential roles to play in the practice of the faith. Love and sexuality are not limited by gender, and same-sex relationships are entirely accepted within the Wiccan community.

Sexual orientation is also celebrated and accepted within Wicca. Wiccans view love and attraction as natural expressions of individual preferences and inclinations. Love, in all its forms, is regarded as a beautiful and sacred aspect of human experience.

In conclusion, love and sexuality in Wicca are celebrated as sacred expressions of life's energies, deeply intertwined with existence's natural and spiritual dimensions. Wiccans recognize the divine aspects of love and sexuality and honor them through rituals, symbols, and ethical principles. The balance between the physical and the spiritual, the celebration of gender equality, and the acceptance of diverse sexual orientations make Wicca a path that embraces the full spectrum of human love and sexuality, fostering a sense of wholeness and sacredness in these aspects of life.

Family and Community Ethics

Family and community play integral roles in Wicca, a modern pagan, nature-based religion that emphasizes interconnectedness and reverence for the Earth. Wicca places a strong emphasis on fostering relationships, both within the immediate family unit and the wider spiritual community. In this section, we will explore how Wicca approaches family and community ethics, the significance of these aspects within the faith, and the principles that guide Wiccans in nurturing connection and responsibility in these contexts.

Within the Wiccan tradition, the concept of spiritual family is highly valued. While many Wiccans have biological families, they also consider their spiritual community or coven as a family form. Wiccans often refer to each other as "brothers" and "sisters" and share a deep sense of connection and responsibility towards one another. This sense of belonging extends to all community members, regardless of biological relationships, emphasizing the idea that spiritual bonds can be just as significant as blood ties.

Respect for autonomy and personal choice is a fundamental principle in family ethics within Wicca. Wiccan parents, for example, often raise their children, emphasizing allowing them to explore and develop their own spiritual paths. While Wicca may be a part of the family's belief system, children are encouraged to make their own choices regarding their faith. This respect for personal autonomy reflects the broader Wiccan ethic of "An it harm none, do what thou wilt," emphasizing personal responsibility and ethical conduct.

Inclusivity and diversity are central to Wicca's approach to community ethics. Wiccan communities strive to be inclusive and welcoming to individuals from diverse backgrounds and belief systems. This inclusivity extends to individuals of different genders, sexual orientations, and cultural backgrounds. Wiccans value the diverse perspectives and experiences that community members bring, recognizing that the richness of the community is enhanced by its diversity.

Interconnectedness and shared responsibility are key principles within Wiccan community ethics. Wiccans believe that all living beings are interconnected, and this belief informs their sense of responsibility towards one another and the Earth. Wiccan communities often engage in environmental initiatives, charitable activities, and support for community members in need. This shared sense of responsibility strengthens the bonds of the community and fosters a spirit of cooperation and mutual support.

Environmental stewardship is a significant aspect of Wicca's community ethics. Wiccans view the Earth as sacred and strive to be responsible stewards of the environment. Many Wiccan communities participate in conservation efforts, eco-friendly practices, and rituals that honor the natural world. This commitment to environmental responsibility is a way in which Wiccans express their reverence for the Earth and their dedication to its well-being.

Celebration of life's cycles is essential to Wicca's family and community ethics. Wiccans mark the changing seasons through Sabbats and honor the moon's phases through Esbats, which are often celebrated as community events. These rituals provide moments of reflection, gratitude, and connection, strengthening the bonds of the community and fostering a sense of shared spirituality.

Conflict resolution and communication are essential skills within Wiccan family and community ethics. Wiccans value open and honest communication highly, encouraging individuals to address conflicts or misunderstandings respectfully and constructively. Conflict resolution is viewed as an opportunity for growth and more profound connection rather than a source of division.

In conclusion, family and community ethics in Wicca emphasize the importance of nurturing connection and responsibility within the spiritual family and the broader community. Wiccans value inclusivity, autonomy, interconnectedness, and environmental stewardship as guiding principles in their family and community life approach. Through their commitment to these ethics, Wiccans strive to create loving, supportive, and harmonious relationships within their families and communities, reflecting their reverence for the interconnectedness of all living beings and the sacredness of the Earth.

The Role of Elders and Teachers

Within the framework of Wicca, a modern pagan, nature-based religion, the role of elders and teachers holds a position of significant importance. Elders and teachers are seen as custodians of wisdom and tradition, responsible for passing down knowledge, guidance, and the spiritual legacy of Wicca to the next generation. In this section, we will explore how Wicca views the roles of elders and teachers, the significance of these roles within the faith, and the responsibilities associated with guiding and nurturing the Wiccan community.

Elders and teachers in Wicca are respected and revered figures within the community. They are individuals who have demonstrated a deep commitment to the faith, extensive knowledge of its traditions, and a strong sense of ethical conduct. Elders often have many years of experience practicing Wicca and have accumulated a wealth of wisdom through their spiritual journey.

Mentorship and guidance are central aspects of the role of elders and teachers in Wicca. They provide support and instruction to newcomers and those seeking to deepen their understanding of the faith. This mentorship can take various forms, including one-on-one guidance, formal training within a coven or circle, or educational workshops and classes.

Preservation of tradition is a crucial responsibility of elders and teachers in Wicca. Wicca strongly emphasizes the continuity of tradition, and elders are entrusted with ensuring that the core beliefs, practices, and rituals of the faith are passed down intact to future generations. Elders often serve as guardians of the Wiccan lineage, responsible for upholding the authenticity of the tradition.

Ethical guidance and leadership are also integral components of the role of elders and teachers in Wicca. They are expected to lead by example, demonstrating ethical conduct, compassion, and responsibility in their interactions with others. Elders often play a key role in resolving conflicts within the Wiccan community, using their experience and wisdom to foster understanding and harmony.

Ritual leadership is another significant aspect of the role of elders and teachers. They are often called upon to officiate at important rituals and ceremonies within the community, such as initiations, handfastings (Wiccan weddings), and celebrations of the Sabbats and Esbats. Their experience and expertise in ritual practice make them essential leaders in the community's spiritual life.

Continued learning and personal growth are also emphasized within the role of elders and teachers in Wicca. While they are often seen as sources of wisdom, elders and teachers are expected to continue their own spiritual journeys and deepen their knowledge of the faith. This commitment to personal growth ensures that they remain dynamic and relevant leaders within the community.

Accessibility and inclusivity are values that many elders and teachers in Wicca uphold. They are often approachable figures within the community, willing to offer guidance and support to individuals of all backgrounds and levels of experience. Elders strive to create an environment where seekers and newcomers feel welcome and valued, fostering a sense of inclusivity and diversity within the faith.

In conclusion, the role of elders and teachers in Wicca is one of great responsibility and honor. They serve as mentors, preservers of tradition, ethical leaders, and ritual officiants within the Wiccan community. Their guidance and wisdom are essential in passing down the rich spiritual legacy of Wicca to future generations. Through their dedication and commitment, elders and teachers in Wicca play a vital role in nurturing and strengthening the Wiccan community, ensuring that its traditions and values continue to flourish in an ever-changing world.

Dealing with Conflicts and Disagreements

Conflict is an inevitable part of human interactions, even within the practice of Wicca, a modern pagan, nature-based religion that emphasizes interconnectedness and community. How conflicts and disagreements are handled within Wiccan circles is crucial to maintaining the harmony and cohesion of the community. In this section, we will explore how Wicca approaches conflict resolution, the significance of dealing with conflicts and disagreements within the faith, and the principles that guide Wiccans in nurturing harmony and growth through constructive conflict resolution.

Wicca strongly emphasizes open and respectful communication as a fundamental principle in addressing conflicts and disagreements. Wiccans value the power of dialogue and believe that honest and compassionate communication is essential in resolving conflicts. This emphasis on communication aligns with the broader Wiccan ethical principle of "An it harm none, do what thou wilt," which encourages personal responsibility and ethical conduct.

Mediation and third-party intervention are often employed within Wiccan circles when conflicts arise. Wiccan leaders, elders, or experienced practitioners may serve as mediators, helping those involved in the conflict to communicate more effectively and find common ground. Mediation allows for an objective perspective and can facilitate a more constructive resolution.

Personal responsibility and self-reflection are key components of conflict resolution within Wicca. Wiccans are encouraged to examine their own role in conflicts and disagreements, taking ownership of their feelings and actions. Self-reflection is a valuable tool for personal growth and self-awareness, allowing individuals to gain insight into their motivations and triggers.

Compromise and finding common ground are often Wicca's conflict resolution goals. Wiccans recognize that not all conflicts can be fully resolved to everyone's satisfaction, but compromise allows for a harmonious and mutually beneficial outcome. Finding common ground emphasizes the shared values and goals that often unite members of the Wiccan community.

Respect for diversity of beliefs and practices is crucial in addressing conflicts and disagreements within Wicca. Wiccans value inclusivity and understand that there is a wide range of beliefs and practices within the faith. This respect for diversity means that disagreements may arise over theological interpretations, ritual practices, or personal spiritual experiences. Wiccans strive to maintain respect for differing viewpoints, even when conflicts arise. Ritual and spiritual practices can also play a role in conflict resolution within Wicca. Some Wiccans engage in rituals or meditations designed to foster understanding, healing, and reconciliation. These practices often draw on the symbolism and energies of the natural world, aligning with Wicca's reverence for nature and the cycles of life. Seeking guidance from elders and experienced practitioners is a common approach when conflicts prove challenging to resolve. Elders and mentors within the Wiccan community often have a wealth of experience in dealing with conflicts and can provide valuable insights and wisdom to those in need. Their guidance is often sought to ensure that conflicts are addressed in accordance with Wiccan principles and ethics. Acceptance of imperfection and growth through challenges is a foundational belief within Wicca. Wiccans understand that conflicts and disagreements are part of the human experience and that they can provide opportunities for personal and communal growth. Through the challenges posed by conflicts, individuals and communities can learn valuable lessons, strengthen their bonds, and deepen their understanding of themselves and their faith.

In conclusion, dealing with conflicts and disagreements in Wicca is guided by principles of open communication, mediation, personal responsibility, and respect for diversity. Wiccans recognize that conflicts are a natural part of community life and seek to address them constructively to maintain harmony and promote growth. Through applying these principles, Wiccans strive to create an environment of mutual respect and understanding within their communities, fostering a sense of unity and shared purpose in their spiritual journey.

CHAPTER X

Personal Journey and Self-Discovery

Creating Your Unique Path

Wicca, a modern pagan, nature-based religion, is often celebrated for its diversity and flexibility, allowing practitioners to create their unique spiritual paths. While Wicca has a rich tradition and a set of core beliefs and practices, it also encourages individuals to explore their personal connections with the divine, the natural world, and the mysteries of existence. In this section, we will explore the concept of creating a unique path in Wicca, the significance of individuality within the faith, and the principles that guide Wiccans in embracing their spiritual journey.

Wicca recognizes that spirituality is a deeply personal and individual experience. It encourages practitioners to explore their own beliefs, connect with the divine in their unique ways, and develop a spiritual practice that resonates with their inner truth. This approach aligns with the Wiccan ethical principle of "An it harm none, do what thou wilt," emphasizing personal responsibility and ethical conduct in all aspects of life, including one's spiritual path.

Exploring diverse traditions and practices is a common way for individuals to create their unique path in Wicca. Wicca itself is not a monolithic tradition but a diverse tapestry of practices, beliefs, and traditions. Some Wiccans may feel drawn to specific traditions, such as Gardnerian, Alexandrian, or Dianic Wicca, while others may choose to incorporate elements from various traditions into their practice. This diversity allows individuals to find the spiritual path that best resonates with their beliefs and experiences.

Connecting with nature and the elements is a central aspect of Wicca, and it provides a rich foundation for creating a unique path. Practitioners often develop a deep relationship with the natural world through gardening, nature walks, or other earth-centered activities. This connection with nature allows individuals to draw inspiration from the cycles of life, the seasons, and the elements, incorporating these themes into their spiritual practice in their way.

Personal rituals and magical practices are essential tools for those forging their unique path in Wicca. Wiccans often design rituals and spells that reflect their personal intentions, goals, and beliefs. These rituals can vary widely, from simple daily devotions to elaborate ceremonies for specific occasions. Personal rituals allow individuals to infuse their spirituality into their daily lives, fostering a sense of connection and purpose.

Exploration of deity and the divine is another avenue for creating a unique path in Wicca. Wicca is often described as duotheistic, with the worship of the God and Goddess as central to the faith. However, the conception of deity within Wicca is diverse and allows for various interpretations. Some practitioners may see the God and Goddess as distinct divine entities, while others may view them as symbolic representations of universal forces. Still, others may connect with entirely different deities from various mythologies. This diversity of belief allows individuals to find a personal connection with the divine that resonates with their spiritual journey.

Personal growth and self-awareness are emphasized within Wicca as individuals embark on their unique paths. Wiccans understand that personal growth is an essential aspect of their spiritual journey, and they often engage in self-reflection, meditation, and other practices to deepen their self-awareness and understanding. This commitment to personal growth allows individuals to evolve and refine their spiritual path continually.

Respect for diversity and inclusivity is a guiding principle in creating a unique path in Wicca. Wiccans value the diversity of beliefs and practices within the faith and recognize that there is no single "right" way to practice Wicca. This respect for diversity encourages individuals to explore their spirituality without judgment and to engage in open and respectful dialogue with others who may have different perspectives.

In conclusion, creating a unique path in Wicca is a deeply personal and empowering journey. Wicca's emphasis on individuality, nature, diverse traditions, personal rituals, deity exploration, personal growth, and inclusivity allows practitioners to forge their spiritual path in a way that aligns with their beliefs and experiences. By embracing their individuality and spirituality, Wiccans can find meaning, connection, and fulfillment on their unique journeys within the rich tapestry of Wiccan practice.

Keeping a Book of Shadows

The Book of Shadows is a central and revered tool within the practice of Wicca, a modern pagan, nature-based religion. It is often regarded as a personal, sacred repository of wisdom, knowledge, spells, rituals, and magical experiences. The concept of the Book of Shadows has evolved over time, reflecting the unique path and practices of each Wiccan practitioner. This section will explore the significance of keeping a Book of Shadows in Wicca, its history and development, and the principles that guide Wiccans in maintaining this treasured book.

The Book of Shadows, often abbreviated as "BoS," serves several essential functions within Wicca. Record-keeping is one of its primary purposes. Wiccans document their magical experiences, rituals, and spells using their Book of Shadows. It becomes a personal journal of their spiritual journey, allowing them to track their progress, successes, and lessons learned along the way.

Preservation of tradition is another vital role of the Book of Shadows. It serves as a repository of knowledge passed down from one generation of Wiccans to the next. Elders and teachers often provide guidance and share their wisdom with newer practitioners, who then record these teachings in their own Books of Shadows. In this way, the tradition is preserved and passed on, ensuring its continuity.

Spellwork and ritual guidance are also central to the Book of Shadows. It contains instructions for performing various rituals, spells, and ceremonies, along with correspondences, chants, and incantations. Wiccans refer to their BoS when conducting magical work, ensuring accuracy and consistency in their practices. The Book of Shadows thus becomes a practical tool for Wiccans in their spellcasting and ritual work.

Personalization and creativity are encouraged in creating and maintaining a Book of Shadows. While there are certain traditional elements that many Books of Shadows contain, such as the Wiccan Rede, the Wheel of the Year, and the principles of magic, each practitioner is free to customize their book to reflect their unique path and experiences. This personalization allows Wiccans to infuse their energy and intention into their BoS, making it a profoundly personal and meaningful reflection of their spiritual journey.

The history and development of the Book of Shadows in Wicca are intriguing and reflective of the religion's evolving nature. The term "Book of Shadows" was popularized by Gerald Gardner, often considered one of the founders of modern Wicca. Gardner's Book of Shadows contained a mix of ritual instructions, spells, and his interpretations of magical practices. Gardnerian Wicca, one of the first Wiccan traditions, closely followed this template.

Over time, the concept of the Book of Shadows evolved. Doreen Valiente, a prominent figure in the early Wiccan movement, significantly contributed to its development. She reorganized and rewrote much of the material found in Gardner's Book of Shadows, making it more accessible and coherent. Valiente's revisions contributed to the spread of Wicca and the development of new traditions.

Today, the Book of Shadows takes on a variety of forms. Some Wiccans maintain handwritten journals or grimoires, while others opt for digital versions stored on computers or in cloud storage. Some practitioners use a combination of both. The flexibility of the Book of Shadows allows each Wiccan to choose the format that best suits their needs and preferences.

Ethical guidelines often play a role in maintaining a Book of Shadows. Wiccans are encouraged to use their BoS responsibly, respecting the principles of the Wiccan Rede, which emphasize personal responsibility and ethical conduct. This ethical approach extends to using spells and rituals recorded in the BoS, ensuring that magic is practiced with harm to none.

In conclusion, the Book of Shadows in Wicca is a cherished and versatile tool, serving as a personal journal, a repository of tradition, a guide for spellwork and rituals, and a canvas for individual creativity. Its history and development reflect the evolving nature of the religion, while its personalization and ethical principles ensure that it remains a significant and sacred aspect of Wiccan practice. The Book of Shadows continues to be a treasured companion on the spiritual journeys of Wiccans, helping them connect with their inner wisdom and the magical world around them.

Lifelong Learning and Growth

One of the core principles in Wicca, a modern pagan, nature-based religion, is the commitment to lifelong learning and personal growth. Wiccans believe their spiritual journey is an ongoing discovery, transformation, and self-awareness process. In this section, we will explore the significance of lifelong learning and growth within Wicca, how Wiccans embrace this journey, and the principles that guide them in their quest for spiritual development.

The pursuit of knowledge is a fundamental aspect of lifelong learning in Wicca. Wiccans are encouraged to explore various topics, including mythology, herbalism, astrology, tarot, divination, and various magical traditions. This quest for knowledge is not limited to formal education but extends to self-directed study, reading, and the exchange of wisdom within the Wiccan community. Wiccans continually seek knowledge to deepen their understanding of the natural world, spirituality, and the mysteries of existence.

Personal experience and self-discovery are highly valued in Wicca. Wiccans believe that spirituality is a deeply personal journey, and they encourage individuals to explore their own beliefs, experiences, and connections with the divine. Through personal rituals, meditation, and introspection, practitioners gain insights into their own spirituality, develop a deeper connection with nature, and uncover their unique path within the faith. This emphasis on personal experience allows Wiccans to forge a profound and authentic connection with their spirituality.

Mentorship and guidance play a crucial role in lifelong learning and growth in Wicca. Experienced practitioners, often called elders or mentors, provide guidance and support to newcomers and those seeking to deepen their practice. Elders share their knowledge, wisdom, and experiences, serving as valuable resources for individuals on their spiritual journey. This mentorship fosters a sense of community and allows for the passing down of traditions and teachings from one generation to the next.

Ritual and magical practice are central to the lifelong learning journey in Wicca. Wiccans engage in regular rituals, ceremonies, and spellwork to connect with the divine, the natural world, and their inner selves. These practices serve as opportunities for growth, transformation, and spiritual exploration. Through the repetition of rituals and the refinement of magical skills, Wiccans deepen their connection to the energies of the Earth and the mysteries of the craft.

Reflection and self-assessment are essential components of personal growth in Wicca. Wiccans engage in regular self-reflection, examining their beliefs, actions, and intentions. They assess their progress on their spiritual journey, identify improvement areas, and set personal development goals. This commitment to self-awareness allows practitioners to continually evolve and refine their understanding of themselves and their spirituality. Community and shared wisdom are valuable resources for lifelong learning and growth in Wicca. Wiccan communities often gather for workshops, classes, and discussion groups, providing opportunities for individuals to learn from one another and exchange ideas. These communal experiences foster a sense of belonging, allowing Wiccans to draw upon the collective wisdom of their peers and engage in meaningful dialogue about their spiritual journeys.

Embracing change and evolution is a core principle in Wicca. Wiccans understand that spirituality is not static but dynamic, evolving as they gain new insights and experiences. This openness to change allows practitioners to adapt their beliefs and practices to better align with their evolving understanding of the world and themselves.

It also encourages them to explore new avenues of spiritual growth and self-discovery.

In conclusion, lifelong learning and growth are integral to the practice of Wicca. Wiccans value the pursuit of knowledge, personal experience, mentorship, ritual practice, self-reflection, community, and adaptability as they navigate their spiritual journey. Through these principles and practices, Wiccans continually deepen their understanding of themselves, the natural world, and the spiritual dimensions of existence. The journey of discovery and growth in Wicca is a profound and enriching one, offering practitioners the opportunity to forge a deeper connection with the divine and the mysteries of the craft.

Embracing the Alchemy of the Spirit

Alchemy of the spirit is a profound concept within Wicca, a modern pagan, nature-based religion. It signifies the transformative process through which individuals seek to elevate their consciousness, develop their spiritual connection, and effect positive change in themselves and the world around them. In this section, we will explore the significance of embracing the alchemy of the spirit in Wicca, the principles that guide this transformative journey, and how Wiccans actively engage in this sacred process.

The essence of alchemy lies in the pursuit of personal and spiritual transformation. Wiccans believe in the interconnectedness of all things and recognize that they can change themselves, their surroundings, and the energy that flows through the universe. This belief is aligned with the Wiccan Rede, which emphasizes personal responsibility and ethical conduct, stating, "An it harm none, do what thou wilt." Within this framework, Wiccans embark on a spiritual quest to transform themselves and their lives in alignment with these principles.

Alchemy of the spirit begins with self-awareness and introspection. Wiccans engage in regular self- examination, seeking to understand their motivations, emotions, and beliefs. By delving into the depths of their consciousness, practitioners gain insight into their strengths, weaknesses, and areas for personal growth. This introspective journey allows them to identify aspects of themselves that require transformation and healing.

The Wheel of the Year plays a significant role in the alchemy of the spirit in Wicca. Wiccans celebrate the cycles of nature through the Sabbats and Esbats, marking the changing seasons and the moon's phases. These rituals provide opportunities for reflection, gratitude, and connection with the natural world. They serve as moments of transformation, allowing individuals to align themselves with the energies of the Earth and the cosmos.

Ritual and magical practice are essential tools in the alchemical journey of the spirit. Wiccans use spells, ceremonies, and rituals to manifest their intentions and desires. These practices harness the power of intention, visualization, and energy manipulation to effect change in the physical and spiritual realms. Through ritual, Wiccans transform their desires into reality and work to manifest positive outcomes.

The concept of the divine and the Goddess is central to the alchemy of the spirit in Wicca. Wiccans often view the divine as immanent, present in all aspects of the natural world. The Goddess, representing the feminine aspect of divinity, is revered for her nurturing and transformative qualities. Wiccans connect with the Goddess in rituals and meditations, seeking her guidance and assistance in their transformative journey.

Community and shared wisdom play an essential role in embracing the alchemy of the spirit. Wiccan communities offer support, guidance, and a sense of belonging to individuals on their transformative path. Elders and mentors provide valuable insights and share their experiences, helping newcomers navigate the challenges and joys of the alchemical journey. The communal aspect of Wicca fosters a sense of unity and collective transformation.

Integration of the shadow self is a crucial component of the alchemy of the spirit. Wiccans understand that personal growth and transformation require acknowledging and healing the darker aspects of themselves—the fears, traumas, and negative patterns. By facing and integrating these shadow elements, practitioners can achieve greater self-awareness and wholeness, leading to profound spiritual transformation. Environmental stewardship and ecological responsibility are integral to the alchemy of the spirit in Wicca. Wiccans revere the Earth as sacred and recognize the importance of protecting and preserving the natural world. Many engage in eco-friendly practices, conservation efforts, and environmental activism as part of their transformative journey. This commitment to ecological responsibility aligns with the belief that personal and planetary transformation are intertwined.

In conclusion, embracing the alchemy of the spirit in Wicca represents a profound and transformative journey of self-discovery, growth, and positive change. Wiccans actively engage in this sacred process through self-awareness, introspection, ritual, connection with the divine, community support, and ecological responsibility. By aligning themselves with the cycles of nature, the energies of the cosmos, and their inner wisdom, practitioners of Wicca seek to elevate their consciousness, effect positive change in themselves and the world, and embrace the transformative power of the alchemical spirit.

CONCLUSION

In conclusion, "A Journey into Wiccan Ethics: Alchemy of the Spirit- Discovering the Transformative Philosophy and Ethics of Wicca" is a comprehensive exploration of the rich tapestry of Wiccan beliefs, practices, and ethical principles. Throughout this ebook, we have delved into the roots of Wicca, its influential figures, and the evolution of its philosophy and ethics. We have examined fundamental concepts such as the Wiccan Rede, the divine and the Goddess, the Wheel of the Year, the elements, and the concept of magic.

Moreover, we have explored the ethical foundations of Wicca, including the Threefold Law, the principles of "harm none" and personal responsibility, and the intricate balance between personal freedom and responsibility. We've discussed the role of karma and the ethical considerations in spellwork.

We've also delved into practical applications of Wiccan philosophy in daily life, rituals, and magical practices. We've addressed controversies and debates within the Wiccan community, various types of rituals, and the use of tools and herbalism. We've examined Wicca's place in contemporary spirituality and its challenges and misconceptions.

This ebook has provided insights into the importance of ecological responsibility, animal totems, and interfaith dialogue within Wicca. We've discussed love, sexuality, family, community ethics, and the role of elders and teachers in the Wiccan community.

Furthermore, we've explored the significance of personal growth, the transformative power of the alchemical spirit, and the importance of embracing change and evolution in Wiccan practice.

In embracing the alchemy of the spirit, Wiccans continually seek personal and spiritual growth while also fostering positive change in themselves and the world around them. Wicca's diverse and dynamic nature ensures that each practitioner can craft their unique path, informed by their beliefs, experiences, and ethical principles.

This ebook has aimed to provide a comprehensive guide to Wicca's transformative philosophy and ethics, offering valuable insights and perspectives for both newcomers and experienced practitioners. It is our hope that the readers of this ebook will find inspiration and guidance on their spiritual journey within the enchanting realms of Wicca, and that they will carry the wisdom and ethics of this ancient yet contemporary tradition into their own lives, fostering positive change and harmony in the world.

Thank you for buying and reading/listening to our book. If you found this book useful/helpful please take a few minutes and leave a review on the platform where you purchased our book. Your feedback matters greatly to us.